PAUL GOLDING

THE FINAL BATTLE

A COMPREHENSIVE EXAMINATION OF 1,400 YEARS OF CONFLICT BETWEEN ISLAM AND THE WEST

JOAN KEEP THE FAITH

ISBN 979-8-89778-068-6

9 798897 780686

CONTENTS

This book is dedicated to the brave activists of 'Operation Fightback' who confronted dangerous Islamists and terrorists under my leadership...

About the author

Paul Golding is a nationalist veteran with over a quarter of a century in the trenches of politics. He is the leader and founder of the Britain First party.

Paul was born in London in 1982 and he first got involved in patriotic politics in 1999. He served as Director of Publicity and Director of Communications for a former political party and was elected as a local councillor in 2009 in Swanley, Kent, becoming the first nationalist councillor in the southeast. Paul is a Christian and in 2011 founded the Britain First movement with a membership of only three individuals. Many years later, under his leadership, the Britain First movement has millions of supporters globally.

The movement he has built has been recognised from Washington to Moscow. Paul has stood in elections for parliament, for local councils and for Mayor of London. Paul was sent to prison in 2016 for confronting a Muslim hate preacher who was secretly recorded saying it's okay for Muslims to keep sex slaves. Paul has been served with official death threat 'Osman Warnings' and jihadists have been imprisoned for planning to behead him. Paul was sent to prison again in March 2018 for 'harassing' a migrant paedophile rape gang in Ramsgate.

Paul is one of the most persecuted patriots in British political history, having been sent to three different prisons, arrested over twenty times, prosecuted over ten times and been dragged to court over thirty times. He has also been harassed by 'S015 Counter Terrorism Command' for political activities. Paul has spent time in HMP Pentonville, HMP Elmley and HMP Liverpool, all for political activities.

While in HMP Elmley, Paul was attacked by an Islamist prison gang and suffered injuries. Despite CCTV evidence, the police refused to prosecute the Islamist attackers. The authorities have tried every trick in the book to try and silence Paul, such as High Court injunctions, probation orders, bail conditions and post-sentence supervision orders. In April 2019, Paul published a book called 'The Battle for Britain', which detailed the horrific suffering, persecution and terror threats he has faced.

Paul is perhaps the most lied about and slandered politician in British political history and has suffered numerous media hatchet jobs to try and destroy his reputation. His official Wikipedia page is riddled with lies. Paul is one of a tiny handful of people around the world who is permanently banned from Facebook, Instagram and YouTube. Despite the constant setbacks, prison terms and social media censorship, Paul has built Britain First to be the most active and most energetic patriot party in Britain.

Paul has risked his life many times confronting dangerous Islamic extremists and convicted terrorists. Paul led a street confrontation campaign against known Islamic extremists - such as notorious hate preacher Anjem Choudary - that resulted in them being driven off the streets. His personal battles with Islamists led him to write this book.

Acknowledgements

I wrote this book over a period of two months starting in late December 2024. I have, however, been wanting to write this book since the beginning of my personal battles with Islamic extremists back in 2014. I simply never got round to it, until now.

Now that I have finished this book, I am immensely proud of it. I set out to write an accessible book that would be the 'go-to' publication for all patriots, nationalists and counter-jihad activists concerning Islam.

I have endeavoured to avoid misinformation about Islam while writing this book. As you will see, I have pointed out many misconceptions and dispelled many myths about Islam while also being frank about the many terrible and dark sides of the religion. I want the reader to understand the truth about Islam, so I have pointed out many of the lies and distortions that are regularly repeated about it. I have tried to be as accurate and truthful as possible while writing this book and will gladly receive any complaints or recommendations from Islamic scholars should they read it.

I would like to thank Ashlea Simon for help with proofing and general advice. She has been invaluable in helping me to get this book finished within a few months of hard work. I would also like to thank Tim Burton, who has helped me enormously with research, source material and proofing. Tim is an encyclopaedia of knowledge about Islam and has pointed out numerous errors in my research, leading to valuable corrections.

I hope you all enjoy this book, and I hope it leads to a deep and meaningful understanding of the religion of Islam. Please read it with an open mind and take onboard the many warnings contained within. I wrote this book with the intention that it would be a serious examination of the 1,400-year conflict between Islam and the Christian West. I hope that when you finish reading it, you will come away with a thorough understand of this pernicious religion.

Paul Golding

1. My battle with Islamists

On 22 May 2013, a terror attack shook the foundations of modern Britain. It was also a life-changing event for me personally. Around 2.20pm in the afternoon, in the town of Woolwich, in southeast London, two Islamic extremists launched a devastating attack on a serving soldier called Lee Rigby. He was rammed with a vehicle while crossing the road, and then they set about him with sharp weapons, almost decapitating him in the process. The attack caused widespread revulsion across the country.

The very next day, I visited Woolwich personally and saw the cordoned off scene of the slaughter. I grew up a few miles down the road in the town of Erith, so I was affected by the attack not just on a political level, but personally too. In the years leading up the attack on Lee Rigby, Islamic fundamentalists were running rampant across the country. A few years previously, they had disrupted a soldiers' homecoming parade in Luton. There were extremist protests and public displays almost every day.

Michael Adebolajo and Michael Adebowale were both known

extremists who worshipped at the mosque in Woolwich. They were radicalised by the high priest of Islamists in Britain, hate preacher Anjem Choudary. The authorities were terrified of tackling this enormous and deadly problem due to fear of being called 'racist'. The authorities turned the other cheek as tens of thousands of radical Islamists displayed their hate on our streets. Endless terror attacks were the result, but the murder of Lee Rigby was the final straw.

The murder of Lee Rigby triggered something in me. As I walked away from the police cordons on 23 May, the day after the attack, something snapped in me. My nation, Britain, needed a man to step forward and do something about the wretched scum that were flourishing on our streets. It was then and there that I resolved to do something to confront and oppose the Taliban scum that were running rampant across the nation.

But what could be done? The police and the security services were determined to do nothing due to political correctness. I accepted that, contrary to all logic and common sense, the police and the security services would probably come down like a tonne of bricks on anyone who dared to combat these Islamist networks. The authorities were on their side, that was the reality of the situation.

As fate would have it, it was during this time that I was engrossed in learning about the Troubles in Northern Ireland. It's just my nature to hop from subject to subject, reading hundreds of books and endlessly learning, and during this time I was learning about the conflict between the Ulster Loyalists and the IRA. What I understand was that, up until approximately 1990, the IRA was running rings around the Ulster Loyalists. The Ulster Loyalists were losing the war, and the IRA was winning.

Then tw men turned the tables on the IRA, Billy Wright (in the countryside of Portadown and Tyrone) and Johnny 'Mad Dog' Adair (in Belfast). How did they achieve this? They copied the IRA's methods and used them against the IRA. Instead of endless – and futile – displays of strength against the IRA on the streets, Wright and Adair launched IRA-style clandestine attacks on known IRA soldiers and leaders, along with Sinn Fein politicians. Wright and Adair launched hundreds of attacks on Sinn Fein/IRA, lasting for years, and put so much pressure on them that they eventually sued for peace. This led to the Good Friday Agreement and the end of the Troubles. Wright and Adair crippled the IRA and pounded them into submission.

This, in my mind, was exactly what Britain needed. Someone to take the fight to the Islamists and make their lives uncomfortable and miserable. Someone was needed to suffocate their activities and render them unable to recruit and radicalise. The alternative was more deaths like Lee Rigby. Something had to be done, and just like Wright and Adair in Northern Ireland, it had to be clandestine, backed up with intelligence, surveillance and hard-hitting operations. The most obvious difference was that we weren't going to wage an illegal terrorist campaign but unleash a wave of legal activities that would deeply unsettle the Islamist networks and their minions.

I recruited a large team of activists and infused them with the new approach. No more futile street protests, we would go after known Islamists at their homes, their workplaces, at their protests and so on. We wanted them to look over their shoulders all day every day for the first time. We wanted to make their lives miserable. After all, these were hate preachers and convicted terrorists. They don't deserve to live in peace! Especially after the slaughter of Lee Rigby. We called this new campaign 'Operation Fightback'.

Thenew recruits were eager to get stuck in, as up to that point, their only outlet to combat radical Islam was endless EDL demonstrations. They relished the opportunity to confront known extremists and terrorists face-to-face. Thankfully, one of these new recruits owned a decommissioned British Army Snatch Land Rover. We took this vehicle, full of activists, into the heart of Islamist strongholds such as Brick Lane in Whitechapel, gaining international media attention. These 'Christian Patrols' in Whitechapel were organised to counter the notorious 'Sharia Patrols' organised by the Islamists, who went around confronting revellers having a good time and homosexuals walking the streets.

The first intelligence that led to a known Islamist was that convicted terrorist, Abu Izzadeen, one of Anjem Choudary's henchmen, was working in a sweet shop in East London. So, we visited this shop and found this mighty warrior of jihad sat on a stool looking like an idiot in a kid's sweet shop. Hardly the public image of a tough convicted jihadist! We returned once again a few weeks later, just to annoy him at his place of work.

Then we found out where Izzadeen lived, and we turned up mob handed with around twenty men to bang on his door. The curtains were twitching, but Izzadeen refused to come out and face us. We returned to his home several times after that, just to make his life a misery. I had a sound system with a microphone and was shouting for him to come out, directly outside his front door. All of his neighbours were watching in disbelief, but once they knew that Izzadeen was a convicted Islamic terrorist, they understood what we were doing. Izzadeen must have been seething with anger, having to be careful at his home and at his place of work.

At this point, intelligence led us to the home address of notorious hate preacher Anjem Choudary. Choudary was the chief spokesman of all the Islamists in Britain. He truly was at the top of the pyramid. I immediately deployed a surveillance team near his home for three days straight. On the third day, my activist watched as Choudary pulled up in a vehicle and went into the property. I immediately mobilised a team of activists who travelled with me to Leytonstone in East London on a dark Friday night.

I always kept information extremely tight with 'Operation Fightback'. No one knew what we were about to do, or what the mission was, until the very last minute. This prevented leaks and police ambushes. Once again, my team of activists had no idea where we were going, but I told them we are going to confront a high-profile Islamist target. They fully understood why we operated like this and accepted it. This approach was critical to maintaining discipline and security. It was a trick I learned while studying the activities of Billy Wright and Johnny Adair in Northern Ireland.

My team and I arrived in Leytonstone, and we parked up several roads away from Choudary's address. It was at this point that I briefed our activists on who we were due to confront. As one unit, we walked the short distance to Choudary's home, but it was completely empty with the lights off. Suddenly, one of our activists screamed 'There he is!' and my activists charged at a small vehicle that had entered the road and was scrambling to turn around and drive off. It was Choudary and his family in the vehicle, and our activists surrounded the car with some jumping on the bonnet.

Choudary was terrified at this unexpected ambush and desperately tried to escape. Our activists did what they could to prevent his departure, but in the end, he managed to get away. Nevertheless, we had achieved what we set out to achieve. The most famous and prominent Islamist and terrorist rabble-rouser in Britain had been ambushed and chased away from his home address. This operation triggered nationwide media attention. It was big news.

That very night, a group called 'Islamic Emergency Defence' issued a warning to me. They declared that if I dared to go near Choudary again, I would be dealt with quickly and harshly. I do not take intimidation lightly, so the very next day, I took the same team of activists back to Choudary's home address and did a Facebook livestream calling on 'Islamic Emergency Defence' to meet me there. We waited a long time, but no one turned up to face us. I decided to go immediately to Brick Lane in the heart of Whitechapel and did another Facebook livestream asking them to meet me at East

London Mosque. Again, no one turned up.

The very next day, I was arrested by the Metropolitan Police for harassment. Choudary went to the police like a coward. The charges were later dropped. Anjem Choudary was moved from the address we turned up at, in Bromley Road, Leytonstone, by the authorities. It didn't take us long to find out where his new address was. The only problem was, we only knew the road he was moved to, not the exact door. So, we began at one end of the road and started knocking doors and showing residents an A4 print out of Choudary's face. After about fifteen minutes, a neighbour confirmed the door he lived at. Mob handed, we knocked at his door, and he emerged wearing his pyjamas, immediately closing the door on us. Choudary was the man who personally radicalised the killers of Lee Rigby, so we kept harassing him at every opportunity.

During this period, Choudary and his minions held regular protests around the Greater London area and at every demo, our activists turned up to confront them. Our activists and I were regularly arrested for charging Choudary's protests. Dozens of Met Police officers would try in vain to block our charge, rugby-tackling our activists to the ground. I remember fondly Choudary's demos outside the Museum of Natural History, on the Bayswater Road and outside the Indian Embassy on the Strand. Every time, we charged their protest, and we were arrested as a result, but we didn't care, as we felt that, for the first time, these Islamist cretins were on the backfoot facing stiff opposition from determined British patriots.

It was at the demo outside the Indian Embassy on the Strand that I confronted a young Islamist by the name of Brusthom Ziamani. I did not know it at the time, but he would later be intercepted on his way to behead a British soldier with a huge knife. When he was arrested and charged, it resulted in worldwide media attention and the footage of me confronting him on the Strand was beamed across the world.

By this point in 'Operation Fightback', our endeavours against Islamists had resulted in millions of views on social media, a gigantic and quote unbelievable following on Facebook (which peaked at 2.2 million), and Britain First becoming a 'household name'. Several TV documentaries were filmed about Britain First, including 'London's Holy War' by VICE. The long-suffering British people were amazed that a group of British patriots had declared war on Islamic extremists and had confronted them with such fearless vigour.

The foot soldiers of 'Operation Fightback' continued to harass and confront Islamists across Britain for several years. We ambushed them at their homes, their workplaces, on the streets and at their protests. By the time the dust had settled, I had been personally arrested over twenty times, prosecuted over ten times and sent to three different prisons. The individual operations and instances of state persecution are too numerous to detail in this book. I have, however, forensically detailed them in the first volume of my autobiography, 'The Battle for Britain'. I strongly suggest that everyone reading this purchases themselves a copy.

I faced extreme personal danger on many occasions while taking the fight to Islamic extremists. I was even targeted by terrorists, and I was completely unaware of the situation! Take, for example, the case of Ummar Mirza and his wife Madihah Taheer, both from Birmingham. They were caught by the police while plotting to chop my head off. They practiced their plan on a dummy, the kind you get in boxing gyms. They both supported ISIS and were deadly serious about chopping my head off. The police completely failed in their duty of care, failing to let me know about a credible 'threat to life'. Instead, I learned about this terror plot against me in the tabloid media! I am sure there were many more plots and plans to kill me out there that I did not know about.

Our exploits against Islamic extremism over the years were truly prodigious. In this chapter, I give a brief outline of some of the actions we took against Islamic extremism, but there are dozens, if not hundreds, more examples I could cite. Order a copy of 'The Battle for Britain' and you can see for yourself how Britain First led a relentless crusade against the Islamists of Britain which suffocated their activities and eventually drove them off the streets. Before 'Operation Fightback', the streets of the UK were awash with Islamic extremism. When 'Operation Fightback' was put to bed, Islamic extremism had disappeared from public view and went underground. I truly believe our fight against Islamism in this country saved lives by disrupting their activities.

My personal battle with these dangerous and fanatical extremists and terrorists led me to study the religion of Islam. I have been researching this religion for many years (on and off since 1999), and with this book, I finally managed to commit all of my learning and study to ink and paper. I must admit, I do not consider myself an 'expert' on Islam, but I know enough, and have enough personal experience, to qualify me to write this book.

To understand the religion of Islam, we must start the very beginning, in the year 610 AD when the prophet Mohammed claimed to start receiving his 'revelations' from 'Allah'. In the next chapter, I will delve into the birth of Islam and its creation by Mohammed in Mecca. In a certain way, I see the publication of this book as a continuation of 'Operation Fightback', bringing the true nature of Islam to the attention of the many people that will read it. I may not be confronting terrorists on the streets of East London anymore, but I can still expose the ideology that radicalised all those extremists.

I am very proud of the bravery shown by the foot soldiers of 'Operation Fightback' and I dedicate this book to their endeavours. I will never forget the dangers we faced together. Not only did we have very menacing Islamic extremists and terrorists to deal with, but the police and the security services who were determined to silence us. We stepped forward when we were needed, and we succeed in driving them off the streets of our country.

2. The birth of Islam

In the year 610 AD, in a cave called 'Hira' in the hills surrounding the city of Mecca in modern-day Saudi Arabia, a man called Mohammed claimed to receive a visit from an angel called Gabriel. Mohammed was 40 years old and up to that point, had lived a quiet life as a middle-class merchant in Mecca. After this initial visit by the alleged angel, Mohammed launched into a life of unrelenting religious zeal, conquest, war and mass murder. The revelations received by Mohammed were eventually committed to ink and paper and became the Quran, the holy book of his new religion, which was called 'Islam'. Mohammed become the central figure of Islam, the 'prophet' and 'messenger' of 'Allah', the god of Islam.

Contrary to the claims of modern-day Islamic representatives, Islam does not mean 'peace'. Islam translates as 'submission'. A good practising Muslim is someone who submits to Allah, the god of Islam. Therefore, the central foundation of Islam is submission to the faith, not any abstract notions of 'peace'. A good Muslim is one who follows the rules and instructions of Islam, via the holy book, the Quran. The Islamic world is known as the 'Ummah', which translates as 'nation' in Arabic. When Muslims hold up their index finger as a gesture, it generally means 'One Ummah', i.e. one single Islamic community. Islam also has its own law code, called Sharia. Sharia Law is very expansive and covers a vast array of subjects. The most infamous parts of Sharia law are its prescribed punishments for various offences, such as cutting off the hands of thieves and stoning for adultery. A Muslim nation run under strict Sharia law is called a 'caliphate', or 'Khilafah' in Arabic, usually ruled over by a caliph, or 'Khalifah'. The most notorious 'caliphate' in recent history is that created by the terrorist organisation ISIS in 2015 in northern Syria and Iraq.

Muslims are also expected to learn about the 'Hadiths', which are the words and actions of the prophet Mohammed. Islam is split into two main groups, Sunni and Shia. The Sunni branch of Islam comprises around 85% of the two groups and is by far the largest. Shia Islam is in the minority, and is strongest in nations such as Iran, Yemen, Iraq and Syria. Shia Muslims believe that Mohammed appointed his son-in-law Hazrat Ali as the first leader of Islam. Sunnis believe the 'caliphs' were the successors of Mohammed. Sectarianism between the groups still dominates the politics of the Middle East.

Contrary to the claims of Islamic leaders and tradition, the Arabs who lived before the time of Mohammed worshipped a god called 'Allah' (one among many). Mohammed did not 'invent' or 'create' the god known to posterity as 'Allah'. There is evidence as early as the first century AD that the Arabs worshipped 'Allah', long before the prophet Mohammed. 'Allah' was just one of many gods worshipped in Mecca, or Arabia, in the centuries leading up to the time of Mohammed. This fact totally negates the Islamic claim that 'Allah' is just the Arabic language translation of the word 'God'.

Contrary to certain claims throughout history, Allah was not a pagan 'moon god' before Mohammed made him the supreme deity of Islam. This claim is widespread, but it is simply not true. The crescent moon symbol of Islam was adopted because of geography. Islam arose in Arabia, where most travel along desert trade routes was undertaken at night, when the only illumination came via the moon. The moon lit the path in front of you, therefore the moon was adopted as the symbol of Islam because according to the early Muslims, the religion of Islam illuminated your path through life as a human. The 'crescent and star' symbolism of Islam was not adopted until much later, under the Islamic Ottoman Empire when they conquered Constantinople.

Many observers claim that Islam is a 'cult', but this is wrong. Islam is a comprehensive religion which governs its adherents totally, controlling their beliefs, mindset, morals, economic life, social life, right down the smallest detail. To dismiss Islam as a 'cult' is to minimise the enormous power and influence it wields over billions of human beings. To dismiss Islam as a 'cult' is to obscure the terrible threat is poses to Christendom and Western civilisation.

In the city of ancient Mecca lay a small stone shrine, called the 'Kaaba'. It is considered the centre of the world by Muslims, and contains a mysterious black rock called the 'Al-Hajar al-Aswad'. All Muslims are expected to pray in the direction of Mecca, regardless of geographical location. It is a widely held belief that the black stone in the Kaaba is a meteorite, but this is not true. Muslims revere the black rock because they claim it was given to Adam when he was expelled from the Garden of Eden. All Muslims are expected to visit the Kaaba at least once in their life, during the Islamic pilgrimage called the 'Hajj'. Before the coming of Mohammed, the Kaaba was a pagan temple. The black stone mentioned before was used in pagan worship before Mohammed. But Muslims claim the Kaaba was built by Abraham, the central figure of Judaism, and his son Ishmael. This claim has no historical or evidential basis. You will recognise the

Kaaba in modern times by the familiar sight of Muslims engaging in 'circumambulation', i.e. walking in circles around the Kaaba in large crowds.

Many 'gods' were worshipped at the Kaaba prior to Mohammed. Mohammed, it seems, simply chose one of the many gods worshipped in pre-Islamic Mecca and built his religion around that chosen deity. As already explained, worship of 'Allah' in Mecca, based around the Kaaba, preceded Mohammed by centuries. All of these incontestable historical facts undermine the classification of Islam as an 'Abrahamic faith', along with Judaism and Christianity. It is the view of the author that Islam is a non-Abrahamic pagan religion, with no intertwining at any point on the historical timeline with Judaism and Christianity.

The religion created by Mohammed did not start with Abraham, nor did it overlap with Judaism and Christianity at any time. It sprung forth exclusively from pagan traditions, centred around a pagan building (the Kaaba), in a pagan city (Mecca), in a pagan land (Arabia). Any claim by Mohammed that his religion was the fulfilment of the Abrahamic covenant was done purely to give his new ideology a veneer of legitimacy and credibility. In other words, Islam does not share the same roots and origin as Judaism and Christianity - it is entirely separate.

A short time after the first visit from the angel in the cave of Hira in 610 AD, Mohammed began preaching to the public in Mecca, attracting a small but loyal band of followers, the world's first Muslims. Due to persistence and unrelenting effort, the number of Muslims grew, until they formed their own armies and waged campaigns of conquest, first subduing the Arabian Peninsula, then the Middle East and North Africa, then parts of Asia and Europe, and so on. In the year 622 AD, Mohammed's public preaching and agitation became too much for the pagan people of Mecca, and he was exiled from the city, moving to the nearby city of Medina. In

Medina, he achieved much greater success, uniting the people of the city under his banner and teachings, including the Jewish tribes of the area, and formed a military force, plotting a return to Mecca.

In 623 AD, Mohammed launched his first military campaign by attacking a trade caravan from Mecca. Thus, the 'first arrows were shot for Islam'. The people of Mecca raised an army to retaliate, and at the Battle of Badr, the Muslims won their first military victory. Mohammed soon fell out with some of the Jews in Medina, expelling them from the city. After multiple battles that ebbed and flowed between the Muslims in Medina and the pagans in Mecca, in the year 630 AD Mohammed conquered Mecca and converted the local people to Islam. Mohammed then set about violently conquering neighbouring tribes and forcibly converting them to Islam. When he died in 632 AD, he was the undisputed warlord and master of all Arabia. These early military campaigns and battles formed the basis of Islamic 'Jihad', i.e. holy war against non-believers. Mohammed set the precedent with 'jihad', and his successors would follow this doctrine to the letter, subjecting vast swathes of the known world to violent Islamic conquest and subjugation

In its wake, over the course of centuries, lay countless atrocities and genocides. Islam is not a religion that can co-exist with other belief systems. With Islam, it is all or nothing. Throughout the centuries following the time of the prophet Mohammed, native populations of invaded lands across Europe, Asia and Africa were given a choice, convert to Islam, or pay the 'Jizya', a tax on non-Muslims to avoid execution and death. By these means, Islam was foisted onto the unwilling populations of three continents. Many, many times Europe came close to falling to Islamic conquest, before being repelled at the gates of Paris, Vienna and so on.

The prophet Mohammed must have been a charismatic and forceful personality. He came from nothing, with no followers, and within a few hundred years his religion was on the verge of world conquest. We must examine the phenomenon that is Mohammed with a clear head, free from passion and bias, and give credit where credit is due. To achieve what he did, he must have possessed great personal qualities. To understand Islam, one must understand Mohammed. According to Muslims, Mohammed is the ideal human being, worthy of emulation. Therefore, as with Christianity and Jesus Christ, Islam rises or falls on an examination of the person that is Mohammed, the central figure upon which the religion is based. It is the author's view that Mohammed was not a prophet, but a false prophet and a fraud. But for the sake of continually pointing this out, I will refer (occasionally) in this book to him as the 'prophet Mohammed'. This is not an endorsement of Mohammed as a legitimate prophet, but it makes life easier when writing – and reading - a book. Muslims consider Mohammed to be a prophet, so I will occasionally refer to him as the 'prophet Mohammed' for ease of writing.

When one examines the birth of Islam, we cannot separate it from war, conquest and subjugation. From the very beginning, the two have walked hand-in-hand. Mohammed's peaceful street preaching in Mecca only led to failure and expulsion. In contrast, his military endeavours while ensconced in Medina led to power, prestige and success. From this arose the concept of 'jihad', which has been the favoured exploit of Islamic rulers for 1,400 years. Millions of innocents have perished in endless jihadist wars and battles. The final death toll would easily be able to compete with that of communism, which hovers around the 100 million mark. From the first arrows fired at the trade caravan from Mecca in the year 623 AD, to the terror attack in Southport in England in 2024, the common denominator is 'jihad', and in-between spans 1,400 years of bloodshed and mass murder. It all originates with the person known to history as the prophet Mohammed, and his religion which sprung forth from the paganism of the Kaaba in Mecca.

If current trends and birthrates continue, then the Western world, from North America to Australia, and everything in-between (discounting a few Slavic nations in eastern Europe), will be fully Islamic within the next 30-40 years. The now deposed ex-ruler of Libya, Colonel Gaddafi, said, 'We have 50 million Muslims in Europe. There are signs that Allah will grant Islam victory in Europe—without swords, without guns, without conquest—will turn it into a Muslim continent within a few decades.' Via the womb and the cradle in the modern age, Islam is advancing where jihad has failed. But Islam and violence cannot be separated, and this tradition goes back to the very beginning outside of the Islamic holy city of Medina where the first Muslims attacked a trade caravan with bows and arrows.

We are left with two inescapable conclusions then when studying the birth of Islam. Firstly, Mohammed is Islam, and Islam is Mohammed. Secondly, Islam has, for 1,400 years, been spread by the sword, by conquest, violence and coercion. Without 'jihad', Islam would still be consigned to the Arabian Peninsula. But thanks exclusively to jihad, Islam pierced as far as Paris and Vienna, leaving in its wake unparalleled destruction and horror. Islam began with Mohammed the man and his blood-stained exploits in Arabia, but after his death, the Islamic steamroller began rolling like an unstoppable force across the Middle East before bursting into Europe and Africa. In the next chapters, we will examine the history of Islamic jihad, conquest and expansion from the death of the prophet to the modern era.

3. The first 100 years of jihad

Contrary to the nauseating - but persistent - claims of Muslims living in the Western world, 'jihad' does not solely mean a personal 'inner struggle'. Jihad can also mean holy war against non-believers. The most common historical form of jihad is the violent conquest or subjugation of non-Muslims. In the modern era, faced with Western opponents who have an obvious technological superiority, jihad often means terrorism against civilians. This is usually accompanied by shrieks of 'Allahu Akbar' ('Allah is the Greatest'). What choice do jihadists have, when facing Western enemies who have aircraft carriers and space programmes, except to attack defenceless civilians

In the modern era, whenever jihadists have faced Western militaries in open combat, the jihadists have been annihilated. This has forced jihadists to focus on sneak attacks on civilians, hence the thousands of terror attacks on non-Muslim targets since 9/11. The word 'jihad' translates roughly as 'struggle' and can mean 'personal inner struggle'. But the most commonly accepted modern perception of jihad is that of violent actions against non-Muslims, so we will stick with that. Violent militaristic jihad is a central facet of Islam and cannot be divorced from it. It is also the duty of all Muslims to wage jihad against non-believers, whether willing or not. The Quran specifically states that Muslims who wage jihad are superior to those who don't.

It was jihad, not preaching or the written word, that gave Islam all of its victories and spread the religion across three continents. It is prescribed in Islam that all of humanity must be converted, one way or another. Therefore, jihad is an endless, open-ended endeavour and will only stop when the whole world has been converted to Islam. Although there is considerable debate among Islamic and non-Islamic scholars on the issue, it seems that certain Islamic scriptures promise those who fall in battle while waging jihad a bounty of 70 or 72 virgins in 'Paradise'. Some commentators say that this was invented by Mohammed to entice his followers to fight his enemies. Some say the original Arabic translations do not promise any virgins and the whole thing is misinterpreted nonsense.

Regardless of whether it is true or not, a large percentage of Muslim jihadists truly believe that should they fall in battle against the enemies of Islam, they will receive a certain number of virgins when they enter paradise. This makes them especially willing to die while waging jihad. Some translations of the words of the prophet Mohammed mention that believers will receive 72 'Houri' when arriving in paradise. The word 'Houri' roughly translates, according to Wikipedia, as 'maiden women with beautiful eyes who live alongside the Muslim faithful in paradise.' According to the Hadiths, the 'Houri' do not sleep, do not get pregnant, do not menstruate, never blow their noses and are never sick. They also have transparent skin (so much so that you can see their bones), are eternally young, generally hairless and have huge round breasts.

It is hard to believe that any intelligent humans can be seduced by this rubbish to die for their faith while inflicting murder and mayhem on others, but millions of Muslims believe it all without hesitation. This mindset produces endless waves of enthusiastic jihadists who desire to die for their religion while waging warfare against non-believers. They truly believe that their souls will travel immediately to 'paradise' where they will each receive their small army of transparent-skinned big-breasted virgins. As previously stated, Mohammed's early preaching in Mecca ended in failure and his exile to Medina. Only when he took up the sword did Mohammed find success. This was the birth of what we know today as 'jihad', and it has not ceased in 1,400 years. In this chapter, we will examine the rapid and violent expansion of Islam from its heartland in Arabia starting immediately after the death of the prophet Mohammed.

The most notable feature of early jihad is its rapidity. In less than one-hundred years after the death of Mohammed, Islam had reached modern day southern France, India, Sudan and Italy. Again, following Islamic doctrine, the conquered populations were given a choice, convert, die or pay the 'Jizya'. The speed and expanse of this conquest is comparable to that of Alexander the Great, although Alexander conquered the known world in only ten years. The first victim of jihad was modern day Iraq, called Mesopotamia in antiquity. Mesopotamia was the 'cradle of civilisation', from the Sumerians to the Babylonians. It was a region that was advanced and wealthy and full of well-developed ancient cities. The Islamic invasion of Mesopotamia was the first campaign outside of Arabia, and in less than a year the entire region had been subjugated. It is notable that during the invasion of Mesopotamia, the Muslims first faced troops from the Eastern Roman Empire (the Byzantines), who had allied with the Persians to fight the new threat from further south.

The next victim of jihad was Persia to the east, known today as Iran. In a lightning campaign the Muslims conquered the whole of

Persia and deposed the last of the Sassanid rulers. The whole region fell to the invading Muslims and the heirs of Mohammed seemed unstoppable. The Muslims then turned West, and set their sights on modern day Syria, which was under the control of the Eastern Roman Empire. The Muslims assembled a huge army. Morale was high due to the successful subjugation of Mesopotamia and Persia. The Eastern Roman Empire was a powerful state and should have been able to resist the Islamic hordes, but this was not the case. In a series of lightning campaigns, battles and sieges, the Muslim army conquered all of Syria, seizing control of Damascus, and sent the forces of the Eastern Roman Empire packing.

The Muslims then seized control of the area known today as Israel, or Palestine (a Roman term for the area created to mock the native Jews). Troops from the Eastern Roman Empire had been cut off in Palestine by the lightning conquest of Syria and couldn't put up much of a fight. The Muslims also seized control of the Lebanon and the Levantine coast immediately after. The region known today as Israel, or Palestine, was populated by Jews, Greeks and Romans during the period of early jihad. The Arabs we know today as 'Palestinians' are only living in the region due to conquest and colonisation that occurred centuries earlier. The Palestinians are not native or indigenous to the region but are invaders and colonisers. The only reason Israel has a Palestinian population is due to jihad which occurred from the 7th century onwards.

With most of the Middle East firmly in their grasp, the Muslim armies turned their attention to the heartland of the Eastern Roman Empire, known today as Turkey. Muslim armies swept into the region and in less than ten years conquered around half of the territory under the control of the Byzantine emperor. The capital city of the Eastern Roman Empire, Constantinople, would hold out for centuries, but gradually, slowly but surely, the Islamic hordes chipped away at the territory of the Byzantines and reduced it to a remnant surrounding Constantinople.

Back in the east, Muslim armies launched new expeditions from their base in Iran, conquering most of modern-day Afghanistan and raiding into Pakistan and India. Pakistan was completely subjugated and its population converted to Islam, but the Hindus of India managed to defeat the Muslims in battle and maintained their independence. A tribe called the 'Kafirs', in a region in northern Pakistan called 'Nuristan', managed to hold out and kept the Muslims at bay, giving rise to an Islamic slur attributed to non-believers, that of 'Khufur'. I have personally been called a Khufur many times by Muslim political opponents. During this period, the Muslim armies attacked the world's first Christian nation, Armenia, in the southern Caucasus, killing tens of thousands and enslaving many more. The Armenians managed to repel the Muslims, keeping their freedom until the arrival of the Muslim Turks many centuries later. The Turks actually originate in a region of Western China and Mongolia and were converted to Islam during the eastern expansion of early jihad. The Muslims managed to defeat a Chinese army of the Tang Dynasty and thanks to this, many areas of Central Asia were converted to Islam. The conversion of the Turks to Islam was to have devastating repercussions for the world hundreds of years later.

With the Middle East overrun and the Byzantines in full retreat, the Muslims then turned their attention to North Africa, using their newly conquered territory of Palestine as a base for the invasion. The city of Memphis was captured after a siege, and so was the city of Alexandria. Again, mirroring previous campaigns, Egypt was conquered without difficulty. Alexandria was home to a huge and famous library, and the local Alexandrians pleaded with the Muslims to spare all the ancient and historical manuscripts. The caliph of the Muslims back in Mecca rejected this request, stating that the Quran was sufficient for all men, and as a consequence the manuscripts were used as fuel to heat the city's baths. This devastating act of vandalism meant that an enormous amount of precious knowledge was lost to mankind forever.

Once their grip on Egypt was consolidated, the Muslims pushed on further along the Mediterranean coast, seizing modern day Libya, Tunisia, Algeria and Morrocco before reaching the Atlantic Ocean. The final stronghold of the Eastern Roman Empire in North Africa, the ancient city of Carthage, fell to the Muslims shortly after. After Carthage fell, the only resistance to Islam came from the Berbers, who had European racial descent, but they were too crushed with brutal violence. The Muslims quickly built a navy and conquered the Balearic Islands of Spain.

It was that this point on the timeline that Islam became a grave and existential threat to Christian Europe. With their grip on North Africa secure, the Muslim armies stared out across the Straights of Gibraltar at the Christian, Visigoth kingdom of Spain, eager to carry their relentless jihad into the heart of Europe. Only nine miles of ocean separated them from Christendom, and they had already repeatedly defeated the Christian armies of the Eastern Roman Empire, the 'Byzantines'. Surely they would find similar success on the European continent? In 711 AD a Muslim army embarked for Europe, landing at Gibraltar. The Muslim advance was unstoppable, capturing city after city, defeating army after army. The Spanish king was killed in battle, and within eight years of fighting, the Muslims had conquered almost all of Spain, leaving just a slim strip of Christian land in the north, in the region we now call the Basque country.

The Muslims renamed Spain to 'Al-Andalusia' and subjected the native people to brutal repression. The occupation was so horrifying that the Muslims demanded that the native Spanish hand over one-hundred white virgins annually for use in Islamic harams or face the consequences. Having conquered and consolidated rule over Spain within a decade, the Muslims then moved further north, crossing the Pyrenees and invading modern day France. The Muslims would launch three separate invasions of France, aiming to conquer Europe. The first invasion of France was launched in 721 AD and turned out to be a complete failure, the Muslims being defeated at the Battle of Toulouse. After receiving reinforcements from North Africa and the Middle East, the Muslims launched their second invasion in 732 AD. After sacking the Christian city of Bordeaux and defeating the local French ruler in battle, the Muslims pressed north towards Paris. Unfortunately for the Muslims, they faced no ordinary king in Charles Martel ('Charles the Hammer'), king of the Franks.

Charles was a warrior king and more than a match for the invading Muslims. He was the right man at the right time to save Europe from Islamic subjugation. At the Battle of Tours in 732 AD, Charles Martel decisively defeated the Muslim invaders, their commander, Rahman, having fallen in battle. After a hard day's fighting, the Muslims fled in the dark of night. Europe was saved, for the time being. The defeat at the Battle of Tours sent the Muslims fleeing back over the Pyrenees and into Spain to rest and re-group. In 737 AD, the Muslims launched their final invasion of France, but were crushed again by the military prowess of Charles Martel and the Franks. Several remaining cities in southern France that were still occupied by the Muslims were recaptured and the Muslims were permanently expelled from French territory. Had any other man other than Charles Martel been king of the Franks at that time, Europe would have fallen to Islam. Charles Martel is without doubt the saviour of Europe. All Europeans owe their existence to him.

Back in the east, the situation was desperate. The Eastern Roman Empire of the Byzantines had lost half of its territory to the Muslim armies, and had retreated back to its magnificent capital city, Constantinople. The first Christian emperor of Rome,

Constantine the Great, had converted to Christianity back in 312 AD and moved the capital of the Roman empire to Byzantium, as Rome was considered too pagan. The Muslims seized all of what is today Turkey and laid siege to Constantinople for the first time between 674–678 AD. The siege was only lifted when the Muslim navy was defeated by the Byzantines used a weapon called 'Greek Fire', which appears to the world's first flamethrower. In 717 AD, the Muslims launched a second attack on Constantinople on land and sea but the walls of the city remained impregnable. The Muslim armies suffered greatly during the harsh winter and when an army of Bulgarian Christians arrived unexpectedly, the Muslims were defeated. In 718 AD, the second siege of Constantinople ended in failure for the Muslims, but they would be back, in even greater numbers.

The second siege of Constantinople concluded the first 100 years of jihad. In less than a century, the Muslims had expanded from the city of Medina in Arabia to the heart of Europe and India. With astonishing speed, all of the Middle East, Asia (as far as China), North Africa, Spain and modern-day Turkey had been conquered for Islam. It was an unparalleled conquest and would have been far more successful had it not been for Charles Martel and the last-minute intervention of the Bulgarians at Constantinople. It was at this stage that Europe attempted to fight back, launching a series of raids and invasions of the Middle East known to posterity as 'The Crusades'. The Crusades temporarily held back the Muslim juggernaut, but only temporarily. We will examine the Crusades, which mostly ended in failure, in the next chapter. After the Crusades subsided, a renewed jihadist offensive would penetrate even deeper into European territory. In its wake, lay some of the worst atrocities in the annals of history.

4. The Crusades and the fall of Constantinople

The first 100 years of jihad were astonishing, starting off in the city of Medina in Arabia and then reaching the far-flung regions of France, India and China. But then the impetus of jihad seems to have dissipated and stalled. Immediately after the first century of rapid progress, conflict between the Muslims and the Byzantines ebbed and flowed, with the Byzantines re-gaining ground in modern day Turkey and Syria, followed by Islamic re-conquest. During this period, the Muslims launched attacks on modern day Greece and Sicily for the first time. For a considerable period, the Muslims and the Byzantines faced off in the Mediterranean, fighting each other to a stand-still.

The first Christian ruler of the Roman Empire, Constantine the Great, had moved the capital city away from pagan Rome to Constantinople, modern day Istanbul in Turkey. Shortly after this move, the Roman Empire split into two segments, with the western capital being established in Rome and the eastern capital remaining in Constantinople. Due to this, a new church emerged, with its headquarters in Rome, known to posterity as the Roman Catholic Church, led by a 'Pontifex Maximus', or Pope. The position of Pope has its roots in Roman paganism, Julius Caesar having been the most famous Pontifex Maximus (chief priest) in previous times, with those occupying this position in ancient Rome having their residence in the Regia building in the Roman Forum. The church based in Constantinople became known as the Eastern Orthodox church.

Faced with relentless attacks from the forces of Islam, the emperor of Constantinople made a plea to the Pope in Rome for military assistance. Pope Urban II heeded the call for help and demanded a Christian army be assembled to assist the Christians in the east. This led to a series of military campaigns known to posterity as the 'Crusades'. It must be stressed that the Crusades were a defensive reaction to the relentless jihad of the Muslims over the previous 400 years. Prior to the Crusades, the Muslims had attacked and ravaged many Christian nations and states. In the modern era, the Crusades are presented by left-wing extremists and Islamists as an immoral attack on peaceful Islamic societies. Nothing could be further from the truth. The Crusades were a response to centuries of jihad.

In 1095 AD, the first Crusade was launched, led by a conglomerate of European Christian nobles. The Crusade penetrated as far as Antioch in Syria, before moving on to the holy city of Jerusalem in Israel further south. After a hard siege, the Christian forces took the city and massacred the Muslim (and Jewish) inhabitants. The Jews had unwisely chosen to fight on the Muslim side, and they paid dearly for this decision. As a result of the conquest of Syria and Israel, several Christian states were created, such as the famous Kingdom of Jerusalem. In response to increased Muslim strength in Syria, the Pope called for a second Crusade, which was led by the King of France and the King of Germany. Their army marched to Jerusalem, but aside from that, and a few failed sieges, the second Crusade achieved nothing of substance.

In 1187, the mighty Muslim warrior and commander known as 'Saladin' managed to recapture Jerusalem from the Crusaders, after a lengthy siege. The history of this period is the subject of a famous Hollywood film called 'Kingdom of Heaven' starring Orlando Bloom. In response to the loss of Jerusalem and the destruction of the Crusader state that ruled over the region, the Pope in Rome once again called on the Christian warriors of Europe to march to the Middle East. This was the third Crusade, and it was led by the most powerful kings of Europe, King Philip of France, King Frederick I of Germany and, most famously, King Richard I of England, known to history as 'Richard the Lionheart'. Richard the Lionheart captured the important coastal city of Acre from the Muslims, and then the Crusaders marched to within striking distance of Jerusalem. Faced with the approach of this mighty Christian army, Saladin prepared to abandon Jerusalem to the Crusaders. It was at this point that Richard the Lionheart decided not to attack Jerusalem but instead negotiated a treaty with Saladin that guaranteed Christians the right to make pilgrimage to the holy city. Thus, the third Crusade ended in failure and the kings and troops headed back to Europe.

The fourth Crusade took place in 1202 AD, with European troops advancing towards the Middle East. Instead of heading for the holy land, they decided to sack the great city of Constantinople and carried off much loot (including the famous Shroud of Turin). Similarly, the fifth Crusade, which took place a few years later in 1215 AD, achieved little, attacking Egypt but then being forced to surrender by the Muslim forces. In 1228 AD, the sixth Crusade was led by the King of Germany, Frederick II, and achieved great success, but only temporarily, having forced the Muslims to give up control of Jerusalem and much of Israel for a period of ten years. In 1243 AD, the Muslims once again stormed Jerusalem, destroying a Knights Templar army and seizing control of Israel. The King of France, Louis IX, organised the seventh Crusade to reclaim the holy land, but this ended in failure, with the king ensconced for most of the Crusade in the Christian town of Acre on the Mediterranean coast.

A few decades later, in 1270 AD, the same Louis IX of France launched the eighth Crusade, but this endeavour was diverted to North Africa and the king died a few months later. The ninth and final Crusade was launched in 1271 AD by the mighty King Edward I (the Longshanks) of England, but apart from the long march to Syria, this Crusade achieved nothing. This concluded the series of military campaigns known to history as the Crusades. The Crusades had some success, especially considering the vast distances and logistics involved, but ultimately, they achieved very little, except to hold back the tide of Islamic jihad for a few centuries. With hindsight, the Crusaders should have focussed their efforts on removing the Muslims from Spain before they marched to the Middle East.

In the decades following the final Crusade, the last Christian strongholds in the Middle East were destroyed, such as Antioch and Acre. The unfortunate Christian inhabitants of those cities were massacred or enslaved. With the conclusion of the Crusades, the Muslims were ready to go on the offensive again. It was at this point in the timeline that the primary strength of the Muslims switched from the Arabs to a new tribe that was migrating west from central Asia, known as the Seljuk Turks. The Seljuk Turks had been converted to Islam when jihadist forces invaded central Asia and attacked China centuries earlier. The Seljuk Turks become infamous for their brutal ruthlessness and countless atrocities. The Seljuk Turks would pick up where the Arabs left off, with even greater success. The Seljuk Turks would become the terror of Europe and Christendom for centuries. The Seljuk Turks stormed into the Caucasus Mountain region from central Asia, proceeding into Armenia and onward into modern day Turkey with a series of lightning campaigns. It was then that the Seljuk Turks founded the 'Ottoman Empire', which would last till the end of the First World War in 1918. Under their leader, called a 'Sultan', the unstoppable Ottoman steamroller carried them through Anatolia to the gates of Constantinople itself.

By the end of the 1300s AD, the strength of the Eastern Roman Empire had been so dissipated and sapped by centuries of Islamic jihad that the armies of the Ottoman Empire had seized all its territories and stood outside the gates of the great city of Constantinople itself. The powerful Sultan of the Ottomans had decided that Constantinople should finally be captured, and in 1453 AD a brutal siege began. In desperation, the Byzantine emperor appealed to the Pope in Rome for assistance, but only a small force was dispatched. Constantinople was on its own. The Ottoman army outnumbered the defenders of Constantinople by ten to one, despite various reinforcements from Europe. The Byzantines were greatly aided by an engineer from Scotland, named John Grant, who helped counteract the Ottoman tunnels they dug under the great walls that surrounded Constantinople.

On 28 May 1453 AD, Sultan Mehmed ordered a huge assault on the city, which, after a night of hard fighting, breached the defensive walls and succeeded in penetrating the city. The Byzantine emperor, Constantine XI, led a final charge against the Muslims in person, falling in battle shortly after. The Muslims finally reached the great church of Hagia Sofia, and enslaved or massacred the civilians hiding within. The Ottoman sack of Constantinople was horrific. The entire population was killed, enslaved or raped.

Many of the inhabitants chose suicide rather than face the wrath of the Ottomans. Constantinople was renamed 'Istanbul' and the mighty Hagia Sofia, built by the first Christian Roman emperor Constantine the Great a thousand years earlier, was converted into a mosque. With the fall of Constantinople, the road into Europe through the Balkans lay wide open. The Ottomans, with customary fury and ruthlessness, would carry their jihad into the very heart of Europe, leaving a trail of genocide in their wake.

5. Renewed attacks on Europe

With the whole of the Middle East, North Africa and modern-day Turkey consolidated and secured by the Ottoman Empire, the Islamic armies renewed their assault on Europe and Christendom. This new wave of devastating jihad would propel the Islamists into the heart of Europe. Only by a whisker did Europe survive. In 1479, a Muslim expedition raided mainland Italy, seizing the town of Otranto in the southeast. The Muslims butchered the entire population, beheading 800 of them on 'Martyr's Hill' outside the town for refusing to convert to Islam. When the Byzantine liberators found the bodies on Martyr's Hill a year later, they placed the skeletons behind glass screens in Otranto Cathedral. They are still on display to his day, a grisly reminder of the Islamic jihad that once ravaged the area.

In Spain, the Islamic occupation lasted 750 years and only ended in 1491. The Muslims never managed to conquer the whole of Spain. A slender territory in the north managed to keep the Muslims at bay, becoming the Kingdom of Leon, and it was from this pocket of resistance that the 'Reconquista' was launched. The Reconquista was a slow and gradual fight back against the invading Muslims. The Reconquista was characterised by back-and-forth attacks and battles, with the Muslims being frequently reinforced from their bases in North Africa. The Spaniards also received reinforcements from across Europe, from as far as Scotland, where James Douglas, a lieutenant of Robert the Bruce, took part in the fighting. Gradually, after centuries of constant warfare, the Muslims were pushed back to an enclave in the south surrounding the city of Granada.

In the 1480s, the Spanish monarchs, King Ferdinand and Queen Isabella, led a campaign to expel the last Muslims from the Iberian Peninsula. In 1491, the final stronghold of the Muslims, the city of Granada, was under siege and after five months of fighting, the Muslims surrendered. After 750 years of incessant conflict, Spain had finally been liberated from the oppressive rule of the Muslims. The Reconquista is an inspirational tale of Spanish Christian determination to topple their jihadist overlords. It also serves as a lesson that hope is never lost, no matter how difficult a situation appears. From a small enclave in the north, the Spaniards fought back for centuries with grit and determination to free their lands. They never gave up, and eventually they won their freedom.

It was in the period preceding the destruction of the great city of Constantinople that the Ottomans launched the first invasion of the Balkans, conquering Serbia, Bulgaria, Thrace, Greece, Albania and Bosnia. Only the city of Belgrade held out against the Ottomans, having been saved from destruction by a Hungarian warrior and hero called Janos Hunyadi. A few years after the destruction of Constantinople, the Ottomans met their match when they encountered a prince from a region called Wallachia (modern day Romania), known to history as Vlad Dracula. Dracula became famous due to his use of terror tactics against the Ottomans. In a single encounter, he would impale some 20,000 Ottoman soldiers on spikes, a sight that terrified the Ottoman Sultan.

In 1897, a famous author called Bram Stoker would pen his iconic work called 'Dracula', portraying a vampire that lived in a castle in Transylvania (part of medieval Wallachia). The character of Dracula was inspired primarily by the exploits of the aforementioned Vlad Dracula, the Terror of the Turks. Vlad Dracula defeated the Ottomans several times over until he was betrayed, and his head was delivered to the Sultan in Istanbul (formerly Constantinople). With Dracula out of the way, the Ottomans finally took Belgrade, marched north into Hungary and took Budapest, and appeared unstoppable. The next target along the River Danube was the great European capital city of Vienna in Austria, which was besieged by a vast Ottoman army of 300,000 in 1529. All of the conquered inhabitants of Budapest had been slaughtered, and this hardened the determination of the fighters defending Vienna who knew that they would be shown no mercy by the Ottomans.

The Muslim army attacked Vienna with brute force but were repelled by the Christian defenders. They tried other tactics to breach the walls, such as tunnelling, but that failed too. As time wore on, disease and dwindling supplies plagued the huge Ottoman army. The Ottomans attacked one last time, but that too was repulsed. Finally, all prisoners taken by the Ottomans were slaughtered and they withdrew further south into the Balkans. Had the Ottomans taken Vienna, then all of Europe would be wide open to them, and Christendom would be fighting for its very existence.

In 1571, the Christians of Europe finally won a great victory over the Ottomans at sea, at the Battle of Lepanto, off the coast of Greece. The victory at Lepanto was overwhelming and led to a huge boost in morale for the Christian cause. For the first time, the Ottoman air of invincibility had been badly shaken. After their failure to take Vienna, the Ottomans invaded the region known today as Moldova and Ukraine. This was significant as it led directly to a war between the Polish and the Ottomans for the first time.

In 1620, war broke out between the Polish and the Ottomans and, even with support from locals in Moldova, the Polish were pushed back. The second war between the Polish and the Ottomans was more successful, with a large Polish army fighting the Ottomans to a stand-still, leading to a peace treaty. Decades later, in 1672 AD, a renewed Ottoman assault forced the Poles to relinquish territory in Ukraine and to pay tribute. The Polish would get their revenge on the Ottomans a few years later.

In 1683, the Ottomans had once again marched another huge army north to the gates of Vienna and began another siege of the city. The stakes were as high as they could be for Europe. The destruction of Vienna would leave central Europe wide open to Islamic conquest. When the siege began, the Ottomans numbered around 180,000, facing off against 11,000 Christian defenders. The Ottomans had previously slaughtered the inhabitants of a village close to Vienna, and this made the defenders determined to fight to the last man. When the Ottoman commander offered the defenders a peaceful surrender, they refused. Therefore, the Muslim attack began, with tunnels being dug underneath the walls of Vienna, a tactic which created several breaches. The situation appeared hopeless for the defenders, and it seemed that Vienna would soon be lost.

It was at this late stage that a miracle occurred. A Polish-Lithuanian army led by the legendary Jan Sobieksi joined forces with nearby Austrian and German troops to form the 'Holy League'. Together, they marched to Vienna and arrived just in time to save the city. The cavalry forces of the Holy League, led by the famous Polish 'Winged Hussars', led a gigantic charge at the Muslims which broke their lines and forced them to retreat. Thanks to the relieving army of the Holy League, Europe was once again saved from the ravages of Islamic jihad. The Ottomans now began a gradual but inexorable retreat south towards Istanbul, being pushed out of Hungary, Serbia, Romania and Bulgaria.

The people of Serbia suffered terribly under brutal Ottoman occupation. Repeated Serbian rebellions were crushed, and thousands of Christians were martyred. The Serbs were so rebellious that the Ottoman commander ordered the heads of Serbian rebels to be mounted on a grisly tower, known to posterity as the 'Skull Tower of Nis', as a deterrence to other would-be insurrectionists. The skulls of 952 Serbian patriots were mounted on the tower, and their scalps were sent to the Sultan in Istanbul. The Skull Tower of Nis is perhaps the most shocking but poignant monument to the brutal genocide inflicted on the Balkans by the barbaric Ottomans.

By the end of the Napoleonic Wars, the Ottomans had been pushed south all the way to Greece, where they lost a decisive naval battle at Navarino in 1827 to a coalition of European navies. Greece finally achieved independence from the Ottomans in 1830 AD, under European protection. The nation of Bulgaria also suffered horribly under the Ottoman yoke, enduring 600 years of occupation and mass murder. As late as the 1800s, the Ottomans were massacring tens of thousands of Bulgarian freedom fighters and wiping out whole villages to deter rebellions. Then in 1877, the Russian Empire of the Tsars declared war on the Ottomans and came to the aid of Bulgaria, and by 1885, the Ottomans had been pushed out of most of the country. Finally, in 1908, only a few years before the First World War, Bulgaria achieved its independence from the genocidal Ottoman Empire.

The Russian war against the Turks had driven them back to the gates of Istanbul itself. Then, the British seized control of Cyprus and Egypt, the French took Tunisia, and the Italians seized Libya. Ottoman power had virtually collapsed, and their empire was reduced to territories in the Middle East. Their reign of terror in Europe, at least, was at an end. The outbreak of the First World War in 1914 saw the Ottomans join the central powers of Germany and Austria-Hungary, which led to the allied nations of Britain and

France attacking them in the Middle East and Turkey itself, such as the Gallipoli campaign.

It was under the cover of the First World War that the Ottomans carried out one of the most savage atrocities in history, the Armenian Genocide. Armenia was the world's first Christian nation and had been a thorn in the side of the Ottomans for centuries. With war raging in Europe, the Ottomans decided to deal with this problem once and for all. Starting in 1915, the Ottomans tried to forcibly move the Armenian population to Mesopotamia. The Armenian population was frog marched for hundreds of miles in every direction, causing them to starve to death and perish in huge numbers. By the end of the genocide, over 1.5 million Armenians had died, and nothing of value had been achieved. The end of the First World War saw the loss of all their possessions in the Middle East and Africa and the end of the hated Ottoman Empire. Turkey became a secular republic under the charismatic Kemal Ataturk, adopted a western alphabet and Islam was sidelined in favour of modernisation. But the scars from 800 years of brutal Ottoman conquest and war left an indelible mark on the Near East and Europe.

It is hard to do justice to the innumerable atrocities inflicted on Europe, North Africa, Asia and the Middle East by Islamic jihadists in just a few chapters of a book. In the last three chapters I have provided a basic outline of the jihad that was unleashed upon the world from its inception in the city of Medina in Arabia. The total death toll spanning 1,400 years of bloodshed is impossible to calculate but could easily reach the 50 million victims mark in my own personal estimation. This would make Islam the second most bloodthirsty ideology in human history, after Communism.

All of this devastating warfare, death and carnage is the result of the endeavours of a single man who lived 1,400 years ago in Arabia, the prophet Mohammed. In the next chapter, we will take a personal look at Mohammed, his behaviour and his personality. According to

Muslims, Mohammed is the ultimate man, to be emulated in every way. Without understanding Mohammed the man, one cannot possibly hope to understand the religion that he spawned, and the blood-stained legacy that resulted from his actions and teachings.

6. The prophet Mohammed

Mohammed was born in or around the year 570 AD in Mecca, in modern day Saudi Arabia, in one of the leading families of the city. His full name was 'Muhammad ibn Abdullah ibn Abd al-Muttalib ibn Hashim'. His father, a man called Abdullah, died before Mohammed was born. Mohammed's mother died when he was six, and he was then cared for by his grandfather, who died when he was eight. He then went to live with his uncle.

His uncle took him on trading missions to Syria and the Levant, but this is about as much as we know of Mohammed's life during his teenage years. A lot of legend has been created around this period of his life, but hard facts and evidence are hard to come by. What we do know, is that Mohammed, under the tutelage of his uncle, became an accomplished merchant. According to the available evidence, Mohammed was a deeply religious man. He retreated to caves outside the city of Mecca for seclusion and prayer on a regular basis. It was during one of these sojourns in a cave (known in Islamic tradition as 'Hira' which is located to the northeast of Mecca) that he received a visit by the Angel Gabriel who began talking to Mohammed in a series of 'Revelations', which later became the Quran. According to Sunni Islam, Mohammed kept these revelations to himself for several years, but according to Shia Islam he immediately set to work to create believers.

The first Muslims were Mohammed's wife, called Khadija, and his close friend Abu Bakr. Mohammed set about preaching in the streets of Mecca, gathering a small following and encountering little resistance at first. He was either mocked or ignored. Mohammed then condemned idol worship and polytheism, and it was then that the factions in Mecca began to turn against him and plot his downfall. One of the main reasons for the pushback from the tribal leaders in Mecca was economic. Mecca was a site of pilgrimage for pagans, and Mohammed's preaching was a threat to this income. Mohammed even encountered resistance from his own tribe, the Quraysh, who guarded the Kaaba in the centre of Mecca, what was to become the number one Islamic holy site. The resistance from the tribes and factions of Mecca reached boiling point and Mohammed and his small following was forced to flee to the city of Medina.

We have already covered most of what happened after this point in the previous chapters of this book that dealt with the history of Islam and jihad, so we will now explore the personality and character of the man who would become the 'Prophet Mohammed' for billions of Muslims. According to Islam, Mohammed was something akin to the 'perfect human being'. This doesn't mean that Muslims consider Mohammed to be sinless. Muslims would say that he had a supreme moral and personal character. He was a man to be emulated in every way. Mohammed was, in other words, the perfect role model for all believers. Whereas Christians regard the Lord Jesus Christ as the perfect model of behaviour and piety, this likewise applies to Muslims vis-à-vis Mohammed.

Any slur or insult of Mohammed in Islam is punishable by

death. There is no negotiation or mitigating circumstances on this issue. Insult Mohammed and you deserve the death penalty. Many Islamic nations dish out capital punishment for blasphemy against Mohammed. This is an interesting issue to dissect, because the logical conclusion derived from this is that to attack Mohammed is to attack the whole of Islam and Allah. That's how highly regarded Mohammed is in Islam. I said previously that Mohammed is Islam and Islam is Mohammed. Never was a truer word spoken, as we say here in Britain. As Christians, we can look to the Lord Jesus Christ and proudly say, he was the most perfect human being to ever walk the earth. No one can ever point to anything bad or sinful in the whole of the Gospel when it comes to Christ. He led a perfect life, without fault. Can Muslims say the same about Mohammed?

This chapter aims to dissect the character, personality and deeds of the Islamic prophet. To understand Islam, you need to understand Mohammed, and everything falls into place like a sword entering a scabbard. Unlike the Lord Jesus Christ, Mohammed did not live a flawless life. Mohammed was, in my opinion, not even close to 'role model' material in any way. To be fair, Mohammed must have possessed tremendous personal charisma to achieve what he did. That is without doubt. But the same could be said of many dictators and despots in history. Forcing yourself on humanity does not equal a good moral character.

In the Christian moral universe in which we Westerners find ourselves, the ultimate crime on anyone's list is 'murder', to end another human being's life. Joseph Stalin was, without doubt, highly intelligent, cunning and transformed Russia from a nation of farmers to a superpower with atom bombs. Nevertheless, he still murdered some 20 million people, oversaw a terrifying police state, built a vast network of concentration camps and perfected a system akin to slavery for hundreds of millions of people. He is rightly regarded as a tyrant, a criminal and murderer. With this in mind - and also noting the Islamic claim that Mohammed was a paragon of virtue - what does the historical record show us? Was Mohammed the saint that Muslims make him out to be? Was he the embodiment of morality? If murder is the worst crime, was Mohammed a murderer?

The short answer is yes, the prophet Mohammed was, by any yardstick, a mass murderer. He ordered many murders during his recorded life and approved of others who killed in the name of Islam or the honour of the prophet. Mohammed executed prisoners of war captured in battle. He ordered the deaths of captured opponents, whether civilian or not, for rejecting Islam. The earliest recorded assassination of a person for opposing Mohammed was as early as 624 AD. The recorded history of Mohammed committing, ordering or condoning murder spans from the beginning to the end of his life. Entire tribes who resisted Mohammed, like the Banu Qurayza, where beheaded and the women and children sold into slavery. Between 600-900 male members of this tribe were beheaded in a single sitting. Mohammed claimed that this massacre was due to a visit by an angel of Allah.

When a group of converts from the tribe of Ukil converted to Islam, but then changed their minds, Mohammed ordered them to be tortured to death. In the year 628 AD, Mohammed ordered a man called Kinana to be tortured so that he would reveal the location of hidden treasure. Mohammed ordered the death of a man, Abdullah bin Khatal, because he wrote poems mocking him. He also ordered the slaughter of a slave girl called Fartana for daring to sing satirical songs about him. Fartana was not the only woman who was killed on the orders of Mohammed. A woman from Mecca called Sara likewise insulted the prophet and was brutally killed.

When others displeased Mohammed, the only way to save their lives was to convert to Islam. This 'get out of jail free card' was used many, many times during the life of Mohammed. The options were stark, convert or die. Under this compulsion, many capitulated and embraced Islam, whether genuine or not. Mohammed ordered his followers to 'kill any Jew that falls into your power', and many Jews were massacred. Mohammed also ordered the death of a man for allegedly committing adultery. The poor man was subsequently stoned to death. Mohammed ordered the deaths or torture of prisoners of war, of woman and children, of apostates, of those who opposed him, of those who refused to convert to Islam, of those who mocked or criticised him, and also to gain economic or financial gain, such as alleged treasure. It took me a measly ten minutes of internet research to find over forty confirmed instances of Mohammed ordering the murder of human beings or condoning their murder. I was taken aback somewhat by the scale of his crimes.

But Mohammed's sadism doesn't end there. Another abominable human tradition, that of slavery, was also indulged in by the prophet. Mohammed did not try to abolish slavery (as is so often claimed), but bought, sold, captured, and owned slaves himself. It must be said that, during his time, slavery was widespread and practiced by all nations, tribes and cultures. But others who lived during his era are not claimed to have been the 'perfect human being', to be emulated. Mohammed did free slaves, such as the African called 'Bilal', but only because he converted to Islam. Mohammed made slavery a permitted tradition within the religion of Islam, but he did state several times in their scripture that slaves should be treated well, or that wrongdoers should be punished by having their slaves emancipated.

If an enemy was defeated in battle, they were permitted to become slaves for their Muslim conquers. Vast numbers of people suffered this fate throughout history. Another way to escape slavery is to pay the 'Jizya' (the Islamic tax on non-believers) who then become 'Dhimmis' and then live in a state of 'Dhimmitude'. Mohammed's successful military campaigns resulted in huge numbers of slaves being taken. During this time, female slaves who were taken by the fighting forces of Islam, the 'Mujahadeen', were forced to submit sexually to their captors. The physical beating of slaves is also permitted. Mohammed took many, many slaves during his lifetime. He also traded them. These facts are not in dispute, they are concrete historical facts.

Slavery is permitted by Islamic scripture, including the Quran and the Hadiths. These scriptures contain many horrifying aspects of Mohammed's career as a slave trader. According to these scriptures, Mohammed demanded one Arab slave in exchange for two black slaves, that he discouraged or thwarted the freeing of slaves, that he claimed that female slaves who have sex can be flogged, that Mohammed gave slaves as presents to his companions, that Mohammed purchased more slaves than he sold, and said that it's permitted for Muslims to marry slaves who are already married, and much more.

We will examine the gigantic and long-running Islamic slave trades that spanned the known world in a later chapter. This chapter aims to focus on Mohammed the man, and his deeds, and it is a matter of historical record that Mohammed was an enthusiastic slave owner and trader. He was also an Arab racist, treating black slaves as worth less than Arabs. He is quoted in Islamic scripture as saying that black slaves from Africa have heads that 'look like a raisin'. So far, we have established that Mohammed was a warlord, a mass murder and a practitioner of slavery. But what about his relationship with the opposite sex? Was Mohammed's 'personal life' a place where we can finally find some personal merit worthy of praise? Unfortunately, not.

By any yardstick, Mohammed was a veracious sexual deviant. Again, it must be stated, Muslims will respond to these incontrovertible facts by claiming I am being unnecessarily abusive towards Mohammed and Islam for the sake of it, that I am 'full of hate'. I would retort that as I am writing these words, I am also researching the topics under discussion from a wide variety of sources which are all in harmony with the core tenets of my statements. Anyone reading this book can Google any of the claims made and see for themselves that they are true and reliable.

Mohammed's 'revelations' during his life were collated and became the 'Quran', the most important Islamic scripture. The Quran, and therefore Mohammed, described the afterlife as a 'Paradise' in which all Muslims would have unfettered access to transparent-skinned virgins, where they would have sex all day and engage in care-free gluttony. Mohammed said that a Muslim man in Paradise will be given the strength of a hundred men to eat, drink and have sex. I have to admit, the Islamic 'Paradise' sounds a lot like a normal day in Ibiza. While Muslims were expected to submit to harsh and rigid sexual conduct on earth (unless it is with non-believers), in 'Paradise' they can engage in turbo-charged hedonism. Consumption of alcohol while alive is 'haram' (forbidden), but in Paradise there will be rivers flowing with wine.

The promise of beautiful virgins in Paradise acts like a magnet for sexually frustrated Muslim men here on earth. Mohammed created a 'Playboy Mansion' for his followers as a reward for obedient service. The Muslim 'Paradise' is like an exotic whore house where Allah promises men can maintain an erection all day long. I find it baffling how any man possessing intelligence cannot see through this utter nonsense. Yet today, two billion Muslims hold fast that this quasi 'Pornhub' Paradise is their final destination after death. It must be remembered that this erotic and carnal 'Paradise' springs forth from the fertile imagination of Mohammed himself.

The prophet Mohammed married somewhere between 11-14 wives during his lifetime, excluding concubines. At the time of his death, he had nine wives. It must be pointed out here that Mohammed forbade his followers to take more than four wives. This was supposedly a command from Allah himself. It's a curious case of 'rules for thee, but not for me'. The most controversial, and famous, of these wives was 'Aisha', who was six years of age at the time of their marriage. According to Islamic scripture, Mohammed consummated this marriage when Aisha was nine years old. Throughout the duration of this book, I have tried to be fair and reasonable, and on this point, it must be stated that marriage to pre-pubescent children was the norm for all of humanity up until the 20th Century. With this in mind, it cannot be said, as is so often the case, that the prophet Mohammed was a 'paedophile' in the modern sense. I have also found no credible evidence in Islamic scripture for the claim that until Aisha was nine years old, Mohammed fondled her by rubbing his penis in between her thighs ('thighing').

What we would describe in the modern age as 'child marriage' was commonplace throughout all of human history in all cultures. The problem is that Muslims consider Mohammed to be the 'perfect human' and therefore, if Mohammed had sex with a nine-year-old back then in the 7th Century, then it should be permissible now in the 21st Century. Allah's immutable values do not change according to the calendar. This is why child marriage is so prevalent across the modern Islamic world. Mohammed was a man of his time, the 7th Century. Therefore, we should not be looking to import the values of that era into modern society if they are so egregiously out of sync. But Muslims do not accept this. If Mohammed did it, regardless of the circumstances, it should be permitted in today's world.

Mohammed also forced his adopted son to divorce his wife, Zaynab, so he could marry her. Mohammed was smitten with Zaynab after visiting his son's house. As it was during the summer months, Zaynab was scantily dressed. The problem Mohammed had was, in Arab culture, a father-in-law is considered to be an actual father, and therefore, technically, Mohammed marrying her was akin to incest. Mohammed then claimed to receive a 'revelation' from Allah which permitted him to marry Zaynab. You might say, 'how convenient!'. This story from Islamic scripture shows that nothing stood in the way of Mohammed and his cravings, and he was not averse to fabricating revelations from Allah to justify his lustful desires.

Mohammed is definitely what would be described today as a 'misogynist'. Mohammed is quoted as saying that the majority of the occupants of the 'Hellfire' were women. Mohammed is quoted in the Hadiths more than once saying that women were 'deficient' in intelligence and religion. This is because they cannot allegedly pray or fast during menstruation. Mohammed said that they 'curse' often and are ungrateful to their husbands. He said women could lead a 'wise man astray'. Mohammed's misogyny towards women caused Islamic societies throughout history to develop highly oppressive systems of rules for women. It says in the Quran that women are to dress modestly so as not to arouse desire in a man. This led to the practice of forcing women to wear barbaric dressings such as the 'burqa' or 'niqab'. However, it is not prescribed in Islamic scripture for a woman to completely cover her face or hair. The burqa and niqab are later man-made innovations.

Mohammed waged more than fifty military campaigns or raids during his lifetime, putting him right up there with Napoleon or Genghis Khan for the prize of 'chief warmonger of history'. In Islamic scripture, Mohammed is quoted as saying that the greatest deed of a Muslim is 'Belief in Allah and Jihad in His cause'. Mohammed certainly took warfare and conquest to another level for the hitherto quiet Arab tribes. He is quoted as saying, 'Lining up for battle in the path of Allah is worthier than sixty years of worship'. Of Muslims who refused the call of jihad, he said they will be 'tortured like no other sinful human' in the depths of hell.

In 632 AD, Mohammed contracted an illness and died five days later. He is buried in the great mosque in Medina. During my political career, I have come across claims that he was poisoned by a Jewish

(Above) Ummar Mirza, the ISIS terrorist who plotted to chop my head off with a rambo knife. He is now serving a long sentence in top security HMP Belmarsh.

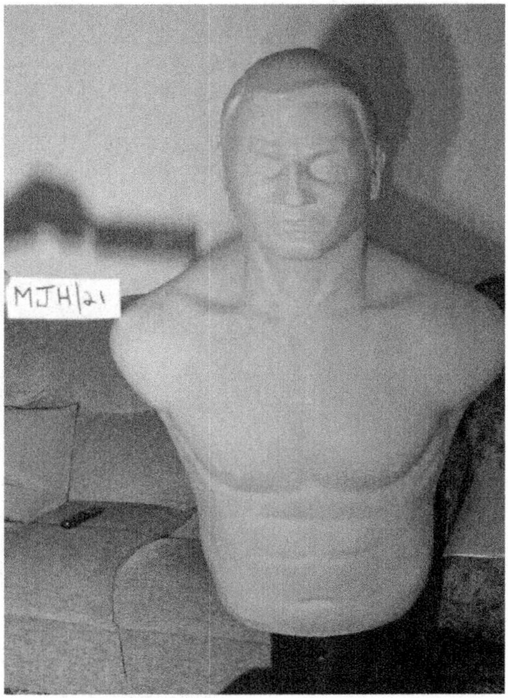

(Above) The dummy that Ummar Mirza and his wife used to practice my decapitation.

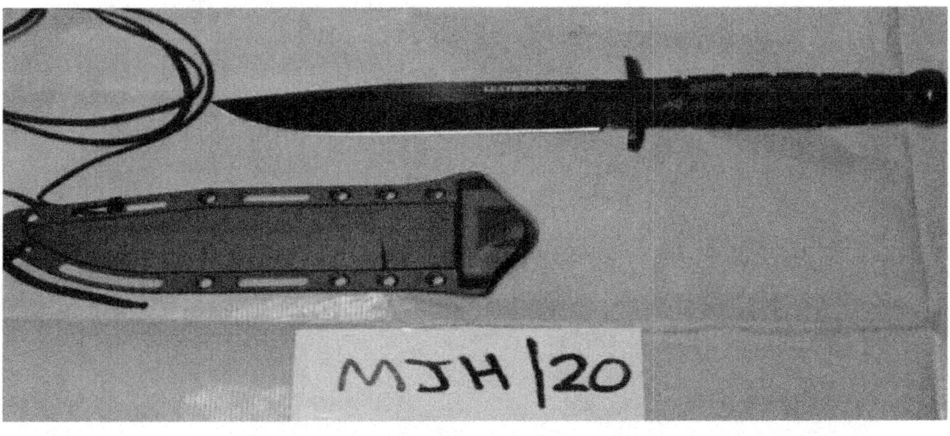

(Above) The huge knife that Ummar Mirza planned to use to behead me. The police are legally obliged to warn me about any threats to my life, but in this instance, they chose not to bother.

(Left) This is the moment Britain First took off. Me and a handful of activists blocking the path of Anjem Choudary in Whitechapel, East London.

(Right) A Britain First activist is wrestled to the ground by the Met Police for charging at Anjem Choudary and his cronies in London.

(Above) Displaying my usual mix of contempt and cynicism towards the politically correct police who allowed the Islamists to operate.

(Above) The famous confrontation between me and Brusthom Ziamani, who was arrested on his way to behead a British soldier.

(Above) A Britain First activist is arrested for confronting convicted terrorists and Islamists in London.

(Above) Islamist Abdullah Deen being protected from our activists by the police. He was forced to flee across the road.

(Above) I have been arrested over twenty times by the police and 'SO15 Counter Terrorism Command' for confronting Islamists.

(Above) A Britain First activist is tackled by the police for charging at hate preacher Anjem Choudary.

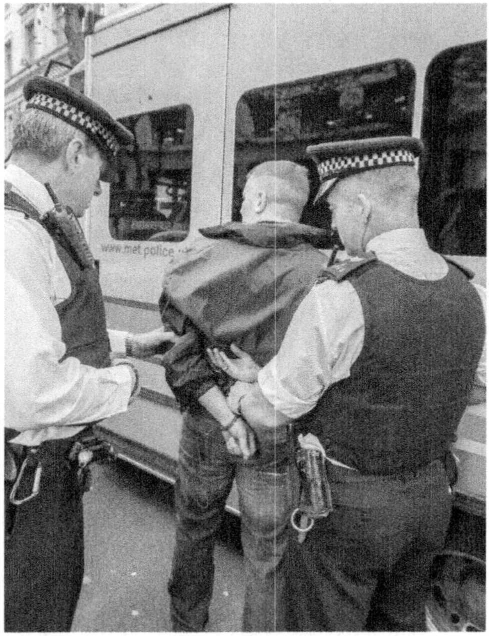

(Above) Another day, another arrest for confronting Islamic extremists.

(Above) The armoured Land Rover we drove at the head of our 'Christian Patrols' in East London. The sight of this vehicle rolling down Brick Lane with our activists either side was incredible.

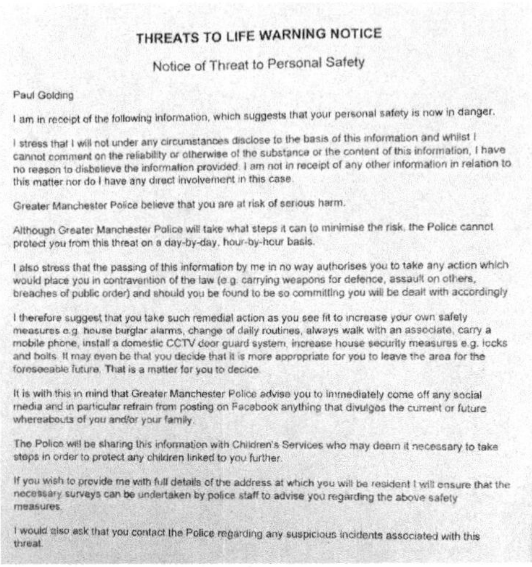
THREATS TO LIFE WARNING NOTICE

Notice of Threat to Personal Safety

Paul Golding

I am in receipt of the following information, which suggests that your personal safety is now in danger.

I stress that I will not under any circumstances disclose to the basis of this information and whilst I cannot comment on the reliability or otherwise of the substance or the content of this information, I have no reason to disbelieve the information provided. I am not in receipt of any other information in relation to this matter nor do I have any direct involvement in this case.

Greater Manchester Police believe that you are at risk of serious harm.

Although Greater Manchester Police will take what steps it can to minimise the risk, the Police cannot protect you from this threat on a day-by-day, hour-by-hour basis.

I also stress that the passing of this information by me in no way authorises you to take any action which would place you in contravention of the law (e.g. carrying weapons for defence, assault on others, breaches of public order) and should you be found to be so committing you will be dealt with accordingly

I therefore suggest that you take such remedial action as you see fit to increase your own safety measures e.g. house burglar alarms, change of daily routines, always walk with an associate, carry a mobile phone, install a domestic CCTV door guard system, increase house security measures e.g. locks and bolts. It may even be that you decide that it is more appropriate for you to leave the area for the foreseeable future. That is a matter for you to decide.

It is with this in mind that Greater Manchester Police advise you to immediately come off any social media and in particular refrain from posting on Facebook anything that divulges the current or future whereabouts of you and/or your family.

The Police will be sharing this information with Children's Services who may deem it necessary to take steps in order to protect any children linked to you further.

If you wish to provide me with full details of the address at which you will be resident I will ensure that the necessary surveys can be undertaken by police staff to advise you regarding the above safety measures.

I would also ask that you contact the Police regarding any suspicious incidents associated with this threat.

(Above) One of the many 'Threats to Life' warnings that I have accumulated over the years.

(Above) The police mugshot when I was sent to HMP Elmley. During this stay in prison, I was attacked by an Islamist prison gang in my cell.

(Above) Seconds after this photo was taken, we were all arrested for charging hate preacher Anjem Choudary who was across the road with his fellow extremists.

(Above) Chasing Islamists Abdul Mahid and Mohammed Rahman down the Bayswater Road in London. Our constant confrontation of these Islamists forced the police to take action.

(Above) Anjem Choudary's bodyguard, Michael Coe, who threatened to cut my head off.

(Above) Convicted terrorist Abu Izzadeen. Abu refused to face me when I was banging on his door.

(Left) The notorious Anjem Choudary, whose life I made a misery with endless harassment. He is now serving life in prison for terrorism.

(Above) Mohammed Rahman, key figure and hate preacher in Anjem Choudary's network.

(Above) White convert Abdullah Deen, who I chased across the road outside the Indian Embassy.

(Above) The Skull Tower of Nis. It was built by the Ottoman Empire in 1809 to deter any further Serbian uprisings.

(Above) Charles Martel ('The Hammer'), the hero and saviour of Europe, at the Battle of Tours in 732. Had it not been for his remarkable victory, Europe would have fallen to Islam.

(Above) Vlad the Impaler, terror of the Ottoman Turks and national hero of Romania.

(Above) Richard the Lionheart, terror of the Muslim and Saladin during the Crusades.

(Above) A Polish army led by Jan III Sobieski arrives at the gates of Vienna to save the city, and Europe, from the Ottomans.

(Above) The Islamic slave trade in Africans was longer lasting, was far more brutal and involved far more Africans than the Transatlantic Slave Trade by Europeans.

(Above) One unfortunate aspect of the Islamic slave trade was the policy of castrating slaves so they could not reproduce. This led to huge death rates.

(Above) Islamic forces took millions of white slaves from Europe. The Barbary Pirates, the Arabs and the Ottomans wrought havoc on Europe, taking slaves from as far north as England.

(Above) Islamic slavers were particularly fond of white European females for use as sex slaves. The harams of the Islamic world were filled up with white European slaves.

(Above) The Kaaba in Mecca, a pagan shrine converted into the most sacred site in Islam. Worship of Allah at the Kaaba pre-dates the coming of the prophet Mohammed.

(Above) The Hagia Sofia in Constantinople, now Istanbul, was once the greatest church in the Christian world. When the Ottomans conquered the city, it was converted to a mosque.

(Above) The destruction of Constantinople was a horrific event, one of the worst slaughters in. The population was massacred and enslaved by the Turks.

(Above) The last Islamic ruler in Spain surrenders to King Ferninand and Queen Isabella. This event marked the end of 700 years of brutal Islamic rule over Spain and Portugal.

(Above) A grisly tower of skulls made up of those slain in battle by the Islamic tyrant Tamerlane in modern day Uzbekistan

(Above) Prince Eugene of Savoy, a great hero of Europe and hammer of the Turks. He helped to relieve the siege of Vienna in 1683.

(Above) Michael the Brave, national hero of Romania, fought bravely against the Ottoman Turks and then drove them out of the country.

(Above) El Cid, who lived in the 11th century, is known as a national hero of Spain. He is remembered as a fierce champion of Christian Spain against the muslim occupation.

(Above) Gjergj Kastrioti Skanderbeg, national hero of Albania, who fought against the Ottoman Empire.

(Above) Janos Hunyadi, national hero of Hungary. Hunyadi's victories made him a prominent enemy of the Ottomans.

(Above) John III Sobieski was King of Poland and Grand Duke of Lithuania. Sobieski was the man who saved Vienna from the Turks.

(Above) Catherine the Great, empress of Russia, Under Catherine, the Russians defeated the Ottoman Turks in two wars.

(Above) Under the cover of the First World War, the Ottoman Turks attempted to exterminate the entire Armenian nation by marching them around the Middle East. This was the first genocide of the 20th Century.

(Above) The Ottoman Empire force marched million of Armenians back and forth, causing widespread death. Around 1.5 million Armenians died. To this day, the Turks deny the atrocity took place.

(Above) During the short lived Islamic State (ISIS) 'caliphate' in northern Iraq and Syria, ghastly atrocities were filmed and published for the world to view. These crimes include burning captured opponents alive, running them over with tanks and mass executions like above. While ISIS shocked modern audiences, their tactics were tyrical of jihadists across the centuries.

(Above) Mega mosque! The Baitul Futuh Mosque in Morden, South London, the largest mosque in the UK.

(Above) Whitechapel tube station, East London, with new signs in Bengali due to the high number of local Bangladeshi Muslims.

(Above) The largest 'Eid' celebration in Europe takes place every year in Birmingham with over 140,000 Muslims gathering to mark the end of the holy month of Ramadan.

(Above) 'Islam will dominate the world' placards are still a common sight in modern Britain. The police refuse to take action.

(Above) White converts to Islam are a huge problem. Approximately 20,000 Britons convert to Islam every year.

(Above) Muslims pray on the streets of East London, despite having a huge mosque nearby. This is universally seen as a show of strength by Muslims.

(Above) Muslims pray in the middle of Parliament Square in central London. There is no reason to do this, except to be provocative and to assert dominance. London is home to dozens of large mosques, but scenes like this are common.

woman, but I have found no credible evidence to support that. Life expectancy during that period of history was short. Life was hard for the vast majority of people, especially in the desert lands of the Middle East. So, I suspect Mohammed simply contracted a sickness, fell ill with fever and died as so many others did. Was Mohammed a good role model for mankind? Taking into consideration all the aforementioned information, he most certainly was not. He was a murder, a slave trader, a sexual misfit, a warlord, a tyrant and a narcissist. He created an intolerant religion of expansion and oppression. Just take a casual look at Islamic societies today, they are all oppressive and backward. As the Lord Jesus Christ said, 'You will know them by their fruits.'

A Muslim may retort, 'What about the UAE? What about Dubai? What about the wealthy Gulf States?' and so on. Well, the 'wealth' of the Gulf States is based purely on oil revenues. Take away the 'black gold' they happen to have in the ground and the whole of Arabia returns to the Dark Ages. Likewise, states like the United Arab Emirates, and even now Saudi Arabia, are increasingly moving away from Islam and embracing modern civilisation without 7th Century superstition. The less 'Muslim' the UAE becomes, for example, the more prosperous it becomes. One can hardly describe modern Dubai as a model of Islamist virtue! It has more in common with Ibiza than the prophet Mohammed.

Mohammed's coming was foretold in the Bible centuries before he was born. The Lord is quoted in the Gospel of Matthew as saying, 'Beware of false prophets, who come to you in sheep's clothing, but inwardly they are ravenous wolves.' To me, this is a clear warning to humanity to be vigilant and to be on the lookout for malefactors like Mohammed, who most certainly was a false prophet. Mohammed's curse upon humanity began in that cave outside of Mecca called 'Hira' where he claimed to receive a visit from an angel. This was also foretold in the Bible many centuries before. In Galatians 1:8,

Saint Paul warned, 'But should we, or an angel from heaven, preach any other gospel unto you than that which we have preached to you, let him be accursed.' Mohammed certainly preached a religion that was the polar opposite of the gospel given to us by our Lord Jesus Christ.

The Lord Jesus never murdered anyone, or waged war, or had sex with slaves, or beheaded captives, or married a child, or tortured someone in pursuit of treasure. The two religions, and their chief protagonists, couldn't be further apart.

7. Islam and Christianity

For Christians, the ultimate authority is the Word of God, the holy Bible. The Bible contains 783,000 words in total across 66 books written by 40 different authors on three different continents which were written over a period of 1,500 years. The Bible starts with the creation of the universe and ends with prophecies of the distant future, and everything in between. The Bible has an incredible level of cross-references and is chronological in nature. Despite the lengthy time period over which it was written, by dozens of authors who had no contact, it is remarkably harmonious and covers a single narrative from beginning to end.

The Quran, by contrast, contains only 78,000 words, which makes it only 1/10 the length of the Bible. The Quran has only one author, allegedly, that being the prophet Mohammed. However, Mohammed was illiterate and did not write the Quran himself. It was written by others after Mohammed's death from accounts he allegedly shared with them. It is not chronological but contains longer chapters at the beginning and shorter chapters at the end.

The Quran contains many of the characters of the Old and New Testaments but changes their names and the details about them. The most obvious would be the Lord Jesus, who the Quran calls 'Isa'. The Quran claims that Isa wasn't crucified, nor did he rise from the dead, nor can he provide salvation. This fanciful adaptation is ignoring a mountain of credible historical evidence. Even the enemies of Jesus confirmed that the tomb in Jerusalem was empty, although they provide alternative theories other than resurrection to explain the empty tomb.

Muslims cannot explain why, in their view, God would wait until 610 AD to revel himself to mankind. It simply makes no sense whatsoever. Mohammed never performed any miracles (acts of God), but the Lord Jesus did. Mohammed never made any prophecies, but the Lord Jesus did. For example, when entering Jerusalem, the Lord Jesus prophesied that the great Temple would be destroyed, 'not one stone will be left standing' (Matthew 24:1-2). A few decades later, the Romans utterly destroyed all the buildings on the Temple Mount. Nothing Mohammed said about the future was ever confirmed by the historical record. This is an important fact to note, because in the case of Christianity, it shows supernatural power at work.

To compare Christianity and Islam, we must return to the origins of both religions. It is claimed that Judaism, Christianity and Islam are all 'Abrahamic faiths', but is this true? I reject this claim profoundly. In my view, only Judaism and Christianity can be called Abrahamic faiths. As we have already covered, Islam has its roots in the pagan worship of Mecca, particularly the Kaaba. Allah was just one of many deities worshipped in pre-Islamic Arabia. But, if we entertain the Islamic claim that their religion has its roots with Abraham in ancient times, we are still left with a huge deficit. The Abrahamic covenant involves a land (Israel), a people (the Jews) and the lineage from Adam all the way up the line to the Lord Jesus, who is the fulfilment of God's promises, the saviour of Mankind. Even the Lord Jesus himself said that 'salvation is from the Jews' (John 4:22), confirming the Abrahamic covenant.

If God's salvation is delivered to mankind through the nation of Israel (the Abrahamic covenant), that excludes the Messiah, messenger or salvation being provided by an Arab, or the Arab nations. This alone invalidates Islam as an Abrahamic religion and demonstrates that it is built on false foundations and lies. Muslims get around this inconvenient situation with a fantastical re-interpretation of the Old Testament narrative. According to Muslims, God's promise of salvation will not come through the nation of Israel, but through Abraham's other son, Ishmael, who is considered the father of the Arab nations. In Old Testament scripture, Abraham's wife Sarah was barren and unable to have children, so she consented to Abraham having a child with an Egyptian servant girl, called Hagar. Hagar gave birth to a son, called Ishmael. But after this, God intervened and said no, despite Sarah's old age, he will ensure that she falls pregnant.

Sarah then gave birth to a son, called Isaac. The descendants of Isaac are what we call today 'the Jews'. The Old Testament is quite emphatic and clear that the promise of salvation will come from the descendants of Isaac (the Jews), not Ishmael (the Arabs). But this didn't stop the founders of Islam from perverting the clear narrative written in the Old Testament. It should be noted that before 610 AD (thousands of years after the life of Abraham) there was no claim whatsoever that the promise of God's salvation would come through the line of Ishmael. Any such claim only appeared with the prophet Mohammed in the 7th Century. The Old Testament actually describes Ishmael as, 'a wild donkey of a man; his hand will be against everyone and everyone's hand against him, and he will live in hostility toward all his brothers.' It is no wonder then that the prophet Mohammed felt an affinity with Ishmael, as this verse could perfectly describe Mohammed himself.

In an attempt to add weight to their 7th Century re-interpretation of scripture, Muslims regularly claim that the Bible has been 'corrupted over time'. In fact, this claim is one of the most important foundations of Islamic thought. I hear this claim on a regular basis. For if Jewish and Christian scripture has been corrupted, then it should not be taken seriously, and Muslims should listen to the Quran only. In 1946, immediately after the end of the Second World War, this claim was blown to pieces with the discovery of the 'Dead Sea Scrolls'. The scrolls showed that the text of the Old Testament has been handed down to us with an astonishing level of accuracy and originality, including the verses where God told Abraham that the promise of salvation would come through his son Isaac, not Ishmael. The Dead Sea Scrolls absolutely nuked any credibility that remained for Islam. It proved that their religion is based on a foundation of lies. The Dead Sea Scrolls demonstrate that Mohammed fabricated the idea that God's promises would be fulfilled through Ishmael in order to suit himself.

When Muslims are asked to prove their claims that the Bible has been 'corrupted over time' by providing the original manuscripts for comparison, they simply can't. Yet they have built their entire religion on this point. The Muslims reject the entire narrative of the Old Testament (the Abrahamic covenant) and the New Testament (revolving around Jesus as Lord and Saviour). They reject it all with ferocious persistency, but at the same time, they can provide no evidential or empirical basis for their own claims. With such shaky foundations, it's no wonder that Islam prescribes the death penalty for leaving the faith. Without capital punishment for apostacy, Islam would have collapsed under the weight of its own nonsense centuries ago.

The Lord Jesus performed many miracles during his lifetime. These miracles demonstrated his dominion over the natural world.

Perhaps the most persuasive evidence we have for the veracity of these miracles is the fact that even the sworn enemies of the Lord confirmed they happened. The religious leaders of His day never denied the miracles took place. The only difference being that they ascribed these miracles to 'magic' instead of his divine nature. By contrast, no divine miracles of any kind were attributed to the prophet Mohammed. Muslims may retort that Mohammed was a prophet and not the 'Son of God', but this ignores that throughout the Old Testament many prophets performed miracles, including Moses, Elijah, Elisha and Isaiah. Mohammed was completely devoid of divine powers.

Mohammed's 'divine' contribution to the world is the Quran, which was handed down to him via hallucinations and dreams and then written up by his followers many years later. There is not a single verse in the Quran that states that the Old Testament or Gospel were corrupted or changed over time. There are, however, dozens of verses in the Quran that confirmed that the Torah (the first five books of the Bible written by Moses), the Psalms of David and the Gospel (the Injeel) were all the word of God. This quandary invalidates the Quran in my opinion. Using basic logic, if the Quran says that the Gospel contained in the Bible is the 'word of God', then why does the Quran contain a radically different narrative and sequence of events? It's a self-defeating logic. The Quran cannot say that the Gospel is true, then provide an entirely different Gospel. It simply doesn't make any sense whatsoever. Mohammed's primary religious contribution to mankind is the Quran, which itself is tiny in comparison to the Bible (one tenth the size), is jumbled and not chronological and contains a vast number of irregularities and inconsistencies. The Quran actually praises Christians for being humble and wise.

The Quran relegates the Lord Jesus to being a prophet only, and not God in the flesh. After all, if Muslims were to accept the overwhelming mountain of historical sources and evidence that confirms the divine nature of the Lord Jesus, then that relegates Mohammed to a 'bit player'. Mohammed would have a much smaller, and subordinate, role in religion. Obviously, that cannot be allowed. Mohammed would not allow himself to be subordinate to anyone. He assigned himself the biggest role available, the 'Messenger of God', more important than anyone who came before him. Muslims also consider him to the final messenger. The story stops with Mohammed.

Perhaps one of the greatest differences between Islam and Christianity is the innate and hostile attitude towards non-believers. It is undeniable that the Lord Jesus preached a message of love towards all of mankind, without exception. The message provided by Mohammed in the Quran is radically different. Muslims have a special word for non-believers, 'Khufur' (or 'Kufr'). This term doesn't only describe non-Muslims. It is derogatory and insulting in nature. The opposite of Khufar is 'Imam', which is the Muslim equivalent of what Christians would call a Priest, Pastor or Vicar, depending on your denomination.

The Quran is virulently hostile to non-believers. The Quran declares that all non-believers will be sent to the 'Hellfire' to suffer for eternity. The verses of the Quran that prescribe hostility to non-believers are called the 'Sword Verses'. It should be noted that the verses of the Quran become more belligerent and bellicose after Mohammed is exiled to Medina. It's almost as if the Quran changes its mood depending on the circumstances Mohammed is facing at any given time. Again, this feeds into the notion that Mohammed was making it up as he went along. There are a number of verses in the Quran that contradict the 'Sword Verses' and are peaceful in nature. Nevertheless, it is widely understood that the Sword Verses (that form the basis of 'Jihad') are superior to the 'Peace Verses'. The Quran is clear that violent Muslims are superior to non-violent

Muslims. For example, Quran verse 4:95 states, 'Allah hath granted a grade higher to those who strive and fight with their goods and persons than to those who sit (at home).'

Quran verse 8:60 advises Muslims 'to strike terror into (the hearts of) the enemies, of Allah and your enemies, and others besides, whom ye may not know, but whom Allah doth know.' Other Sword Verses are equally as explicit in ordering hostility to non-believers. Quran verse 9:29 instructs Muslims, 'Fight those who believe not in Allah nor the Last Day, nor hold that forbidden which hath been forbidden by Allah and His Messenger, nor acknowledge the religion of Truth, (even if they are) of the People of the Book, until they pay the Jizya with willing submission, and feel themselves subdued.' The 'People of the Book' referred to in this verse are Christians and Jews. The 'Jizya' is the Islamic tax on non-Muslims. The Quran stipulates that the only way to co-exist with Muslims is for non-believers to pay this humiliating tax. The only other choice is to convert to Islam or face the violent consequences.

The Quran is made up of chapters (Surah) and there are numerous examples of passages that prescribe violence to non-believers. Here are a few examples:

Surah 3:151: 'We shall cast terror into the hearts of those who disbelieve (all non-Muslims) …'

Surah 2:191: 'And kill them (non-Muslims) wherever you find them … kill them. Such is the recompense of the disbelievers (non-Muslims).'

Surah 9:5: "Then kill the disbelievers (non-Muslims) wherever you find them, capture them and besiege them, and lie in wait for them in each and every ambush..."

This kind of innate malevolence towards non-believers is not found anywhere in the Bible. The Lord Jesus preached that Christians should love our enemies not attack them and chop off their heads. One only has to take a peek at the thousands of Islamic terror attacks worldwide since 9/11 to appreciate how the Sword Verses of the Quran are being applied universally by legions of jihadists on every continent. Islamists never rest, they are always on the attack, because the Quran commands Muslims to be jihadists. Anyone denying this is a deceitful liar and a scoundrel.

Why then do some Muslim representatives claim that Islam is a 'religion of peace'? We encounter this disinformation regularly on television and the wider media. Put simply, Islam permits lying to non-Muslims if it serves the interests of Islam. It's a concept called 'Taqiyya'. Taqiyya is primarily a Shia Muslim doctrine, but it is practiced by both the Shia and Sunni branches in varying degrees. In Christianity, great emphasis is placed on telling the truth, even if it incurs great personal sacrifice. I can quote Proverbs 12:22, 'Lying lips are an abomination to the Lord, but they that deal truly are his delight.' But Muslims are permitted to lie to non-believers, the Khufar.

Muslims regularly bend over backwards to justify their jumbled 'religion'. One example of this is their declaration that Biblical characters that lived centuries before the time of Mohammed are also 'Muslims'. Have a conversation with an average Muslim and they will claim that Adam, Moses and Jesus are all Muslim. They justify this by claiming that, in their view, a Muslim is one who submits himself to God. They cannot see how ludicrous this assertion is. If we accept that criteria, then the author of this book is also a Muslim! Of course, I am not. I am a Bible-thumping, Protestant Christian, a follower of the Lord Jesus Christ.

In summation then, we can see that there are enormous moral and theological chasms between Islam and Christianity. One only has to look at the obvious dissimilarity between Islamic and Christian societies to appreciate this fact. If I were to offer you a choice between moving your family to America, or Afghanistan, it's pretty obvious which you would select. The same could be said for

Britain or Pakistan, Australia or Bangladesh, Canada or Iran, New Zealand or Palestine. The answer is always obvious.

This reality is reinforced by the fact that millions of Muslims are always seeking to leave their Islamic homelands and migrate to Christian, Western nations. The traffic is never the other direction. Millions of Muslims have left Muslim lands and settled in Western nations, only to form their own ghettos and, in some examples, 'no-go zones', where we see regular calls for Sharia Law to be implemented. It could be said that, if they loved Sharia Law so much, they would have stayed put in their Islamic nation of origin. But instead, they 'voted with their feet' and moved to countries which are distinctly non-Muslim. This speaks volumes for the harsh reality of life under Islam.

8. Bizarre facets of Islam

This chapter could be the most important in this book. If the religion of Islam is 'true', then it should not fear a rigorous and all-encompassing examination. Certain parts of Islam should not need to be hidden away from the world. The whole belief system, if really sent down to us by the creator of the universe, should be flawless and perfect. In this chapter, we will examine some of the most fantastical beliefs held by Muslims, taken straight from Islamic scripture.

According to Islam, the prophet Mohammed flew on a winged horse or donkey creature called 'Buraq' from Arabia to Jerusalem where he met with Abraham, Moses, Jesus and other prophets at the Temple Mount. This fanciful story established Jerusalem as the third most important site in Islam. According to this story, Mohammed led those mentioned above in prayer. But that is the end of the story. Mohammed then ascended into heaven where he met with Jesus, John the Baptist, Joseph, Idris, Aaron, Moses, and Abraham and received the command to pray the 'Salat' five times per day. This is why Muslims pray robotically five times every day without fail.

It is sometimes claimed that Mohammed travelled on the winged 'Buraq' creature to the moon, but this is not true. It is also not true that Mohammed split the moon into pieces and then reassembled them. Both of these claims are baseless.

However, it is a core part of Islamic belief that Mohammed flew on a creature to Jerusalem, led a bunch of Biblical figures in prayer on the Temple Mount, then ascended into heaven and back. It is this fantastical fairy tale that forms the basis for the Islamic attachment to Jerusalem. The Muslims later built a mosque on the Temple Mount, the 'furthest mosque', or 'Al-Aqsa', which is a large building with a black dome on the southern end of the platform. They also built a shrine called the 'Dome of the Rock' on the exact site of the ancient Jewish Temple that was destroyed by the Romans in 71 AD.

In Quran 2:73, Allah commands a man to use a piece of cow's meat (a steak) to strike a dead body and bring the man back to life. This was done to prove Allah's power to raise people from the dead. In Islamic scripture, it says that Muslims will be fighting against the Jews, and that trees and rocks will start talking, and they will help the Muslims identify if a Jew is taking cover behind the tree or rock, 'O Muslim, here is a Jew behind me; come and kill him.' I find it hard to reconcile a serious and credible religion with the idea that rocks and trees will leap into action to help Muslims kill Jews.

It would seem that elsewhere in Islamic scripture, rocks get up to more mischief. According to a certain Hadith, the ancient Jewish leader Moses (who the Muslims call 'Musa') was taking a bath, and he placed his clothes on a large rock. According to this Hadith, the rock ran away with Moses' clothes! How naughty. Moses pursued the stone saying, 'My clothes, O stone! My clothes, O stone!' Once Moses caught up with the rock, he proceeded to 'beat' it. 'By Allah! There are still six or seven marks present on the stone from that excessive beating'. It seems the rock got what it deserved. Hopefully the rock won't do anything like that again.

While we are on the subject of Moses, there's another bizarre story one could tell about him from the Hadiths. Allegedly, Allah sent the 'Angel of Death' to Moses, but Moses wasn't happy about this, so he slapped the angel so badly it ruined one of his eyes (an early example of 'F*** around, find out'). The Angel of Death returned to Allah very upset about his treatment, 'You sent me to a slave who does not want to die.' Allah was cross with Moses, so he mended the angel's eye and sent him back to Moses once again, saying 'Go back and tell him [i.e. Moses] to place his hand over the back of an ox, for he will be allowed to live for a number of years equal to the number of hairs coming under his hand.' Moses, it seems, doesn't have any luck in Islamic scripture. First, he had his clothes stolen by a thieving rock, then he gets a visit from the 'Angel of Death'. Perhaps Moses lost his temper over all this, and that's why he decided to give the angel a good hiding. Poor Moses, you can almost feel sorry for him.

It wasn't only humans who suffered the wrath of the bloodthirsty prophet Mohammed. Pet dogs have also suffered considerably due to his malignant influence. While ensconced in Medina after his exile from Mecca, Mohammed was confused why he hadn't received a visit recently from the Angel Gabriel. Mohammed suspected that this was due to a dog that lived inside his house! Naughty dog! Not one to procrastinate, Mohammed then ordered his followers to scour the streets and homes of Medina killing all the dogs they could find. The only dogs that were spared were those used for hunting and guarding land. 'Surely now the angel will visit me!' he must have said. Faced with widespread revulsion across Medina at the unnecessary slaughter of canines, Mohammed then retracted the order. Unfortunately, though, this incident left Mohammed with a permanent disdain for dogs. He still ordered all black dogs to be slaughtered regardless.

Another Hadith provides a barmy story about some villagers

who asked the prophet if they should take water from a well for ablution (ritual cleaning) even if the water had been contaminated by disgusting animal remains or human waste. Mohammed replied that, yes, it is okay, as water cannot be contaminated by anything! 'It was said: O Messenger of Allah, you perform Wudu [ritual cleaning] from the well into which the bodies of dogs, menstrual rags and garbage are thrown? He said: Water is pure and it is not made impure by anything.' It is a scientific and medical fact that contaminated water is the number one cause of disease. This cranky story from the Hadiths is another example of how Islam is wildly out of touch with established scientific fact.

Mohammed could be described as a 'trend setter' during his time. In fact, many of the rules in Islam were established purely by his whims and fancies. Take gold rings for example. One Hadith describes how the prophet acquired a shiny gold ring to wear. But then his followers began to buy their own gold rings, imitating their beloved prophet. Never one to act impulsively, Mohammed then threw away his gold ring and vowed never to wear it again! His followers then began to do the same. Poor Mohammed could never get any peace.

Mohammed 's whimsical decrees also reached into the bedroom. Mohammed prohibited humans from sleeping on their bellies because, according to him, that's how people sleep in hell. 'Do not lie like this, for this is how the people of Hell lie.' Fair enough, we'll just have to sleep on our backs from now on. God forbid we should turn over during the night while unconscious! Mohammed's curses be upon us! While we are on the subject of sleep, Mohammed has some other words of wisdom for us. According to the prophet, if you miss any obligatory prayers during the day, then Satan will camp out inside your nose while you sleep and piss in there all night! When you wake up, according to the prophet, you should wash your nose a minimum of three times, to get rid of all the mess left by

Satan. That seems like excellent advice, thank you Mohammed.

One cannot understate the amazing medical insights found in Islamic scripture. For example, while in Medina, the prophet advised members of the Ukl and Uranah tribes to drink camel urine to ease their discomfort. This Hadith has created a situation whereby camel urine is a widespread medicine used across the Middle East. Camel urine is considered 'Halal' in Islam (permissible). Anyone fancy a nice cold pint of premium camel piss? The prophet was also a pioneer in the art of dining etiquette. Mohammed instructed his followers to eat and drink in a very specific way, 'When any one of you eats, let him eat with his right hand, and when he drinks, let him drink with his right hand, because the devil eats with his left hand and drinks with his left hand.' This is very bad news for those who are naturally left-handed.

According to the Hadiths, Allah loves bad breath when his followers are fasting. During the holy month of Ramadan, Muslims can experience bad breath due to fasting. This is brought about by dehydration, which reduces saliva production. Nevertheless, Allah, it is written, finds this bad odour pleasing, even more pleasing than aftershave or perfume! Each to their own, we suppose. Islam also forbids clapping for men, because that is something that men did in the 'Age of Ignorance' (Jahilliyah), i.e. before the coming of Islam. A better alternative to clapping is apparently shouting 'Takbir' or 'Allah Akbar' (both of which mean 'God is great!') Imagine that at the opera or watching a talent show on a transatlantic flight!

'Zina' is an Islamic term to describe sex outside of marriage. Another, more familiar word, to described this to non-Muslims, would be 'adultery'. But did you know that Zina applies also to animals in Islam? In one particular hadith, it describes how a group of monkeys were seen stoning a donkey to death for having sex outside of marriage. Damn those promiscuous donkeys! Get the monkeys in there to sort them out. It seems that monkeys were the original Islamic morality police.

We are going to have to cut short this never-ending examination of the bizarre facets of Islam, lest this book would grow to an unreadable length. There are, of course, far more passages from the Quran and Hadiths we could talk about. In fact, I could write an entire book that looks exclusively at the weird and wonderful aspects of Islamic scripture. Cramming them all into a single chapter of this book has been difficult, so I have chosen a good sample of examples that illustrate my assertion that Islam is, by any yardstick, a strange and peculiar religion. It must be remembered that all of these odd and anomalous beliefs stem exclusively from the mind of the prophet Mohammed himself. The Quran was given to us by Mohammed, and the Hadiths are stories about Mohammed given to us by people who knew him. With this in mind, Mohammed could be described as a very eccentric and aberrant character indeed.

In Islam, there is a big problem reconciling scripture to reality, as we have demonstrated with the contents of this chapter. If a Muslim is forced to choose between scripture and known scientific fact, the Muslim will always choose his scripture. If you ask your average Muslim if he truly and sincerely believes that Mohammed flew on a winged donkey to Jerusalem, he will say yes, without blinking. Muslims would have no problem confirming any of the uncanny stories mentioned above, regardless of how ridiculous, absurd and laughable they are.

This book aims to comprehensively explore the religion known to us as 'Islam. The objective of this specific chapter is to force the reader to think long and hard about the veracity of Islam. Outside of the core tenets of Islam we are all familiar with, the story of Mohammed, the worship of Allah, the Quran and the Hadiths, the Five Pillars, and so on, are an encyclopaedia of peripheral beliefs that are, quite frankly, bonkers. Regardless of our personal view of these risible beliefs, some of which we have explored in this chapter, they are held as sacred 'truth' by nearly two billion Muslims across the world today. The Islamic idea that Mohammed is the final prophet of Allah is held in equal esteem to the story that a large rock ran off with Moses' clothes while he was taking a bath.

We have to examine the religion of Islam as a comprehensive belief system, not just cherry pick parts of it and ignore others. If you cannot bring yourself to believe that Satan will spend the night in your nose endlessly urinating while you sleep, for missing prayers, then you should call into question whether Mohammed himself was a messenger of Allah. The authenticity of Islam rises and falls on all of its component parts. It has to be accepted, or rejected, as a single monolithic belief. You cannot believe in some parts of it but reject others as barmy. With everything outlined above ringing in your ears, can you honestly say that Islam is a serious, legitimate and valid religion? Take a long, hard think about it.

9. Islamic slave trades

Slavery is central to the history of Islam. From the genesis of Islam in 7th Century Arabia to the present day, slavery features prominently across the ages. The prophet Mohammed bought, sold, captured, and owned slaves himself. Mohammed even married a slave woman. Mohammed gave slaves to his followers as presents. Mohammed decreed that forced sexual intercourse with captured female slaves was permissible. He also declared that Arab slaves were worth two black African slaves. Slaves in Islam were used in social and economic settings. Slaves in Islamic societies were known as 'Jarya'. Life was hard for Islamic slaves, and this led to many rebellions, such as the Zanj Rebellion of 869–883 AD. It should be strongly emphasised that slaves predominantly came from outside of the Muslims world, the 'Ummah'. Converting to Islam was a sure way to escape slavery. Muslim believers could not be enslaved.

The Arab caliphates of the Middle East organised vast and long-running slave trades through Egypt in black Africans, which, according to reasonable estimates, trafficked 6-10 million of them into Islamic lands. This was called the 'Trans-Saharan Slave Trade'. It has to be said that the Trans-Saharan Slave Trade was longer lasting, more brutal and involved much higher numbers of black slaves that the more well-known Transatlantic Slave Trade into the Americas run by Europeans. Also, whereas the Transatlantic Slave Trade lasted approximately 400 years, the Trans-Saharan Slave Trade and its derivatives lasted approximately 1,200 years.

Alongside the Trans-Saharan Slave Trade, we could mention the 'Red Sea Slave Trade' which ran from ancient times to the 1960s (the time during which Saudi Arabia abolished slavery under American pressure). During the period of the Red Sea Slave Trade, Muslims transported black slaves across the Red Sea and into Arabia from modern countries such as Eritrea, Ethiopia, Somalia and Sudan - the Horn of Africa. This trading route ran alongside the Islamic 'Indian Ocean Slave Trade', which supplied black slaves from Africa to the Middle East and as far as Pakistan and beyond. It is thanks to this slave trading route that many areas of southeast Asia have large black populations, all the descendants of African slaves. By the time of the Crusades, towns further south in Africa, in modern day Tanzania, became wealthy centres of the Islamic trade in black slaves. Estimates of the total number of slaves taken via the east coast of Africa through the Indian Ocean are difficult to calculate, but a conservative number would be 8 million. This is a separate number entirely compared to the 6-10 million slaves traded through the Trans-Saharan Slave Trade further north.

The total number of black African slaves taken by the Islamic powers could therefore be as high as 20 million, maybe more. This compares with estimates of 15 million black slaves taken during the European-led Transatlantic Slave Trade to the Americas. It has to be remembered that the prophet Mohammed himself was a racist and referred to black Africans as having heads like raisins. He also considered black slaves as being worth half that of an Arab slave.

It is, therefore, no wonder that Islamic societies looked down on black Africans and viewed them as acceptable and appropriate slave material.

You could ask then, why doesn't the Islamic world have large black populations, like North America? There is a concrete reason for this. The castration of slaves so they could not breed was established practice in the Islamic world. This also led to a horribly high death toll. Huge numbers of slaves who were castrated died after the procedure. The Ottoman Empire in particular was notorious for castrating their slaves. According to various sources, there has a considerable genetic impact on the Arabs due to the presence of huge numbers of African and European slaves. This is to be expected, although the influence of racial mixing was severely curtailed by the practice of castration by the Muslims.

It wasn't until the 20th Century that Islamic nations began the process of outlawing slavery. They did this against their will, having come under immense pressure by Western powers such as Britain. Slavery in the dying Ottoman Empire wasn't outlawed until 1924, when the moderniser Kemal Ataturk took power. Mauritania in northwest Africa became the final Islamic nation to abolish slavery in 1981. Slavery is so intertwined with the history of Islam and Islamic societies that jihadist groups in the Middle East and North Africa have tried to revive it in recent years. There are now slave markets in Libya once again thanks to the fall of Colonel Gaddafi. ISIS was notorious for enslaving hundreds of thousands of non-Muslims, such as Kurds, Assyrians, Chaldeans and Yezidis. So many European slaves were taken by the Islamic nations that the word 'slave' itself is a derivative of the word 'Slav', who are the white inhabitants of Eastern Europe. The Ottoman Empire was infamous for enslaving vast numbers of Europeans. 'Saqaliba' is an Islamic term that refers to slaves subjugated in Europe. Due to the geographical location of the Ottoman Empire and its provinces, the native populations within those areas were white European. The Ottoman Empire enslaved millions of white Europeans during their relentless wars and conquests.

The Ottomans fully understand and appreciated the high intelligence levels of white Europeans, enslaving vast numbers in the Balkans and Eastern Europe and forming them into an elite within their empire to help administer and run that empire. These became known to history as the 'Janissaries'. Kemal Ataturk, the great reforming leader of modern Turkey, was a Janissary (he had blue eyes and fair hair). Vast numbers of female Europeans would end up as sex slaves in the harams of the Ottomans across Southern Europe.

When the Muslims conquered North Africa and parts of Southern Europe, such as Spain, Islamic pirate fleets were formed, and these became known to history as the 'Barbary Pirates'. They were notorious for launching raids on unsuspecting coastal towns and villages, a far afield as Ireland, England and Iceland. Operating from bases along the North African coast, such as Algiers and Tripoli, they terrorised European and Christian ships in the Mediterranean. Over one million white European Christians were captured by the Barbary Pirates and sold into slavery across the Islamic Ummah. The scourge of the Barbary Pirates was so horrendous that the coastlines of Spain and Italy were massively depopulated by people moving inland to escape being captured. The huge and impressive walls of the Vatican City were built primarily to defend against raids by the Barbary Pirates. In 1631, the village of Baltimore in Ireland was attacked by the Barbary Pirates, who took away the entire population back to Africa to be enslaved. English slaves were taken away by the Barbary Pirates after launching lightning strikes in Cornwall and Devon. The Barbary Pirates tormented the Western world as late as 1830.

The Barbary Pirates even attacked ships belonging to the

United States of America. In 1786, famous American leaders such as Thomas Jefferson met with representatives of the Barbary Pirates in London to enquire why they were hostile to American ships. The response was chilling. It was reported back in America that, 'It was written in their Quran that all nations which had not acknowledged the Prophet were sinners, whom it was the duty of the faithful to plunder and enslave, and that every Muslim who was slain in this warfare was sure to go to paradise. He said, also, that the man who was first to board a vessel had one slave over and above his share, and that when they sprang to the deck of an enemy's ship, every sailor held a dagger in each hand and a third in his mouth, which usually struck such terror into the foe that they cried out for quarter at once.'

Faced with the threat from the Barbary Pirates in the Mediterranean and Western Europe, both the Royal Navy and the US Navy took decisive action, lasting many decades. Both navies hammered the Barbary Pirates until they were stamped out. The Royal Navy bombarded Algiers in 1816 and 1820 and attacked Barbary Pirate ships wherever they were found. In a series of conflicts, known as the Barbary Wars, both the Royal Navy and the American fleet severely curtailed the power of the pirates. The Barbary Pirates were finally wiped out when the French conquered Algeria in 1830. This long standing, brutal and evil Islamic slave trading empire finally met its end at the hands of determined Christian naval powers.

The Islamic Ummah was put under considerable pressure by the Christian West to cease and outlaw the practice of slavery in the 20th Century. One wonders whether slavery would still be rife across Islamic lands had the West not intervened. I personally suspect that it would be widespread in Africa and the Middle East. A cursory look at the history of Islam shows us that they never budge from what they believe to be acceptable unless faced with overwhelming pressure from an outside source. The total number of slaves taken by Islamic powers over the course of 1,400 years is very difficult to calculate. We have already arrived at a rudimentary figure of 20 million black slaves subjugated by the Ummah. After researching the subject extensively, I would put the total number of white European Christians enslaved by Islam at 5 million, whether by the Arabs, the Ottomans or the Barbary Pirates.

Left-wing establishments in Western societies place great emphasis and focus on the Transatlantic Slave Trade, trying to induce a feeling of 'White Guilt' into modern populations. But the Islamic slave trades were markedly larger, longer running and far more brutal and sadistic than anything that Europeans organised. It could be said, with a strong degree of accuracy, that Europeans were 'amateurs' when compared to slavery in the Islamic world. Yet Western societies face requests on a regular basis for them to pay 'reparations' to black people, with no such reciprocal calls upon Islamic nations.

To end this chapter, we must remember that Islam specifically and emphatically permits the practice of slavery. Slavery is 'Halal' in Islam (permissible). By contrast, Christianity is vehemently opposed to slavery. It was thanks to Christian abolitionists such as William Wilberforce, the Royal Navy and the British Empire that slavery was eventually stamped out across much of the world. To their eternal shame, many Europeans did engage in the slave trade over many centuries. But when compared to the far more numerous Islamic slave trades, this was a 'blip', a temporary deviation from established cultural and religious norms in the Christian West.

The Lord Jesus never enslaved people, nor did He sell or trade slaves, nor did He subjugate anyone. But the prophet Mohammed leaves us a blood-stained legacy that involves slavery as an Islamic tradition that has been emulated many times down the centuries and still is today across certain parts of the Muslim world. If you doubt me, travel to the Libyan town of Benghazi and enjoy a sunny afternoon in the local slave markets.

10. Islam and the West

It is not an exaggeration to say that since the birth of Islam in the 7th Century, there has been 1,400 years of interminable conflict with the Christian West. We have explored this unabating friction in earlier chapters. Far-left extremists and their Islamist allies like to paint a false picture that it was the West that sparked this antagonism by launching the Crusades. This ignores centuries of previous Islamic jihad attacks on Christian nations in the Middle East, North Africa, Spain and France. The Crusades were a defensive measure in response to hundreds of years of Islamic aggression.

It is also not an exaggeration to say that millions of European and Near East Christians have died in battle - or as civilians - across the ages against belligerent Islamic forces. Countless atrocities took place all around the Mediterranean world long before there was any talk of a Crusade. Yes, some minor atrocities were carried out by Crusaders during their incursions into the Middle East, but these are dwarfed by the apocalyptic death toll inflicted on Christians – and other religious peoples – from Portugal to China, by the followers of

Mohammed, over 1,400 years of constant warfare.

Which brings our examination of Islam to the modern age. It is true that after the fall of the Ottoman Empire at the end of the First World War, Islam entered a period of 'hibernation' which lasted roughly up to the terror attack of 9/11 in New York. During this period, from 1918 to 2001, Islamic extremism was a small and fringe affair across most of the world. Islam was in fact in retreat, having been sidelined in Turkey under the moderniser Kemal Ataturk, in Syria by the Assad dynasty, in Iraq by the secular Ba'athist regime led by Sadam Hussain, and so on. It wasn't until the 'Arab Spring' - which started in 2010 – that the pendulum began to swing the other way and radical Islam started to emerge from the wreckage of secular, political regimes across the Middle East and North Africa. It absolutely baffles the mind why Western establishments encouraged and support this Islamist revival, but they did.

Of course, the most significant development post-Second World War was the opening of the immigration floodgates in the West. What began as a trickle became a flood! At the time of writing in 2025, Europe is home to an estimated 60 million Muslims, maybe more. It is worth quoting the deposed Libyan dictator Colonel Gaddafi once again: 'We have 50 million Muslims in Europe. There are signs that Allah will grant Islam victory in Europe—without swords, without guns, without conquest—will turn it into a Muslim continent within a few decades.' Indeed, Muslims in Europe form a strong and monolithic block which asserts itself politically.

It is important for readers of this book to understand the Islamic concept of 'Hijrah', which in Arabic means 'migration' or 'emigration'. The prophet Mohammed is quoted as saying in a Hadith, 'Whoever migrates with an intention for Allah and his messenger, the migration will be for the sake of Allah and his messenger…' The first 'Hijrah' in Islamic history is of course the migration from Mecca to Medina when Mohammed and his small band of followers were kicked out of the city. Many modern commentators have applied the term 'Hijrah' to the enormous immigration of Muslims into Western lands. Whichever way you look at it, Mohammed's words in the aforementioned Hadith must be borne in mind, that if Muslims emigrate to the West to spread Islam, that is a worthy thing to do according to their ideology. This of course explains why Muslim never integrate into Western society but simply create parallel communities that are segregated.

Focusing on Britain, there are many examples of this. We could cite towns such as Bradford, Luton, Blackburn and so on. If we focus on big cities, such as Birmingham, we could cite areas such as Alum Rock, Small Heath or Sparkbrook. Muslims never intersperse among the native population or among other ethnic minorities. They concentrate, and create their own communities. This is a quintessential example of 'Hijrah', where Muslims emigrate to non-Muslim lands and then create enclaves within those lands. The aim is never to embrace a new way of life, but to spread Islam. When the prophet Mohammed and his followers left Mecca and settled in the city of Medina, they did not adopt the customs of their new city. They did not try to 'fit in'. They agitated and promulgated Islam until they completely dominated their new home and eradicated every other belief system. In other words, they came, they saw, they conquered. This is classic 'Hijrah', and it is happening all across the Western world as you read these words.

By means of 'Hijrah', tens of millions of Muslims have settled across the Western world. Instead of adopting Western values and customs, they cling tightly to Islam and agitate for more Islam. Western society is expected to accommodate Islam, not the other way around. Western societies feature endless Islamic demands for more compromise. If these petulant demands are refused, then the advocates of Islam will hurl their most potent weapon at their deniers, the dreaded word 'Islamophobia'. All and any criticism of

Islam, no matter how justified, is immediately met with screeches of condemnation, and the word 'Islamophobia' is tossed around like confetti. Regardless of the circumstances, Muslims will act as aggrieved victims. Western politicians live in terror of the word 'Islamophobia' and typically capitulate without a fight in the face of Muslim demands. Faced with this system of bullying, vast areas of Western nations have become strongholds of Islam, with not even a whimper emanating from native political leaders.

The petulance and assertiveness of Muslims in Western lands is directly commensurate with their percentage of the population. Generally, when Muslims comprise only 1-2% of any given population, they are quiet and discreet. When that population percentage rises to around 10%, that society will experience a range of negative problems and issues, such as grooming gangs, Sharia courts, prison gangs, Halal slaughter, public broadcast of the Muslim call to prayer (the 'Adhan'), Sharia patrols, widespread mosque construction, calls for blasphemy laws, honour killings, cousin marriages and inbreeding, regular terror attacks, segregated communities, Islamic-issue political candidates, and much more. When the percentage of Muslims exceeds 20%, that nation will fracture almost completely into rival and disparate societies. As the percentage of Muslims increases - mainly due to traditionally high birthrates and mass immigration – the problems increase until finally there is open strife. This societal pattern can be found in the history books in many instances.

Europe is not immune to this model of societal disintegration in the modern area. In Bosnia, the rise of Islam was met with resistance from the native Christians in that region. The result was open and bloody conflict that claimed the lives of many. A bit further south, Albania Muslims migrated into the neighbouring Serbian region of Kosovo in such numbers that eventually they came to dominate the area demographically. The result was a bloody conflict with the native Serbs. NATO decided to intervene in 1999 with an intensive bombing campaign of Serbia. This led to the breakaway of Kosovo from its mother country. Kosovo is a perfect example of the dangers inherent with 'Hijrah' if it is allowed to proceed unchecked. The conflicts in Bosnia and Kosovo should have demonstrated the folly of allowing massive, uncontrolled immigration of Muslims into Europe, but such is the left-wing ideological preference of modern Western political elites that they are blinded to the dangers. They instead prefer to embrace communist doctrines such as 'multiculturalism' and 'diversity', while burying their heads in the sand, instead of learning from 1,400 years of historical conflict between the West and Islam.

At the time of writing, in early 2025, the issue of Islam is of major importance in most Western nations. The 'Clash of Civilisations' between the Christian West and Islam is being felt across North America, Europe and Australasia. Not a month goes by without a major Islamist terror attack or the emergence of another scandal such as 'grooming gangs'. In one way or another, the native populations of the West are feeling the pinch when it comes to Islam, and it is only going to get worse. No hope can be seen on the horizon because mass immigration is increasing, and the birthrates of native Europeans are falling rapidly. This means that the percentage of Muslims across the West is increasing rapidly and without check. In my personal, humble opinion, this process of demographic change will end in tears. Thanks to the stupidity of modern left-wing politicians, we face the prospect of civil war in the future, just like in Bosnia and Kosovo.

Perhaps the most prominent feature of Islam in Britain is the scourge of 'grooming gangs' who prey upon underage non-Muslim girls for sexual exploitation. Across Britain there is an epidemic of child grooming, sexual abuse, rape, and exploitation. Girls as young as eleven are falling victim to gangs who, in many cases, ply them with drink and drugs before passing them around as if they were pieces of meat. Some poor children have been used by man after man, night after night, for years. Lives have been ruined, and lives have been lost. In many cases it's dozens of girls being exploited, and yet for decades the police and authorities have done nothing to stop it. Fear of being accused of 'racism', and an obsession with maintaining an illusion of 'community cohesion' came before protecting British children. The victims are mainly underage, white British girls, although the Sikh and black communities have also been targeted. The offenders are Muslim men, often of Pakistani origin, spanning all age groups. Many cases feature married men, with children of their own, abusing countless young girls, in many instances girls have fallen victim to dozens, if not hundreds of men. They have suffered something which no child should ever suffer, and they have been betrayed.

The authorities turned a blind eye for years, even decades, trying to keep a lid on it the scandal. Many of those in charge still seek to deny that there is a problem at all or admit that there is one but claim that it is not a 'cultural' or 'religious' issue, conveniently ignoring the fact that the victims are always non-Muslim. Huge numbers of Muslim men believe that British children are fair game, easy meat, there to be used and exploited. British children can be raped and abused, in several cases we see victims described as 'white slags' or 'Khufar bitch'. They are treated with utter contempt, used and despised. A high value is put on the virginity of Muslim women until marriage. They are 'off limits'. British and Christian women and young girls, being Khufar, are not. They are fair game, to be used and exploited without a thought for their wellbeing. They are little more than meat, perhaps less since none of them are considered as Haram (forbidden), rather they are all just there to be taken advantage of as non-Muslims. This attitude towards non-Muslim women is what creates the evil of Islamist grooming. To them, British children and women are followers of a lesser God, to be treated with contempt, used and abused without a thought.

Even in cases where children or parents complained of rape and abuse, nothing was done for years, even decades. In some cases, the parents were arrested by the police authorities to silence them. While in Telford, Britain First co-leader Ashlea Simon managed to wheedle it out of the chief inspector of the local police that they have over forty years of evidence of Islamist grooming gangs. It has been stated by Lord Pearson in the House of Lords that the number of victims could be as high as 250,000.

Another prominent feature of Islamic communities in Britain is their refusal to integrate. Muslims have been accused of established their own segregated areas, where the British way of life is non-existent. Instead, Muslims in many of our towns and cities have re-created mini versions of Pakistan on British soil. An example of this parallel society is the creation of a parallel Muslim legal system, centred around 'Sharia Courts'. According to media reports, there are over one-hundred known Sharia Courts operating across the UK dispensing justice according to Sharia Law. Many of these institutions have been mired in scandal, taking the side of husbands in domestic abuse cases for example. This parallel legal system should have been shut down long ago, but political weakness and fear of a Muslim backlash paralyses British politicians.

In our prisons, Islamic gangs have been allowed to consolidate enormous power and influence. Across our prison network, Islamic gangs are such a serious problem that there has been talk of creating segregated prisons that will house Islamic prisoners only. Should a non-Muslim prisoner end up in a fight with a Muslim prisoner, he can expect the retaliatory wrath of all the Muslim prisoners in that establishment. Mess with one, mess with them all. They 'stick together' as one formidable and singular unit. I myself have been attacked in my prison cell by an Islamic gang during my stint at

HMP Elmley on the Isle of Sheppey in Kent. I warned the prison staff of the impending threat, only to be ignored. Finally, despite CCTV evidence, Kent police decided not to press charges for violent assault, letting my Muslim attackers off the hook 'Scot free'. No doubt they were terrified of being called 'racist' so instead ignored a blatant act of criminality. Many hardened British prisoners have converted to Islam purely to keep Muslim gangs off their backs. Radicalisation is widespread in our prisons. Inmates are bullied and harassed into converting to Islam, while the authorities look the other way. The situation is wildly out of control, but the politically correct authorities do not care.

Elsewhere, barbaric ritual slaughter installations dot the British mainland, subjecting animals to horrific and painful deaths. 'Halal slaughter' has become a major political issue. British supermarkets are increasingly hosting special sections for Halal meat and other products. Schools, prisons and other public sector establishments are quietly serving Halal food. Halal slaughter involves the brutal slaying of an animal while an imam recites an Islamic prayer. The poor animal is left to bleed to death. In a nation of animal lovers, such as Britain is, Halal slaughter would be banned immediately. However, legal exception is enshrined in British law. Halal ritual slaughter continues unabated. Videos and photos of Halal slaughter are enough to make a hardened man wince with shock.

Britain is now host to around 1,500 mosques, and this number is growing rapidly. These vary in size, from residential houses converted to places of worship to gigantic 'mega mosques' that can accommodate thousands. This pattern is the same in all Western nations and shows no signs of slowing down. As the percentage and number of Muslims grows, the number of mosques grows in unison. Many mosques have been mired in scandal, preaching extremist concepts such as sex slavery and jihad against non-believers.

I have personally been sent to prison for entering a mosque

to confront a notorious hate preaching imam. This particular mosque, in Cardiff, gained notoriety for pumping out recruits for ISIS when that organisation held sway over northern Syria and Iraq. An imam at the mosque was secretly recorded telling worshippers that it is okay for Muslims to keep sex slaves, because the prophet Mohammed kept sex slaves. When I took a Britain First team to the mosque to confront this imam, he wasn't there. Nevertheless, I was arrested and sent to HMP Pentonville for four weeks for trying to confront him. The establishment in fact sued me in the High Court and I was forced to accept a five-year injunction banning me from entering mosques in England and Wales and the town of Luton, a hotbed of Islamist extremism!

Many mosques in Britain have been the subject of extremism scandals. For example, when a member of the Didsbury Mosque in Manchester attacked an Ariana Grande concert at Manchester Arena with a nail-bomb, killing many, including many children, the mosque was accused by the families of the victims of failing to adequately 'challenge extremist ideology' in the years before the attack. Another example would be a preacher at a mosque in Bradford who called for apostates who denounce Islam to be 'killed' and said Jews and Christians 'cannot be our friends'. We could go on for an eternity detailing further examples of extremism that has been uncovered at mosques in the UK, but that would need a book all of its own to do the subject justice. These few examples should suffice to illustrate the point.

In areas of the UK where the Islamic population dominates demographically, the mosques in that area blast out the call to prayer (the 'Adhan') without any consideration for non-Islamic locals. We expect the Adhan to be blasted out from mosques in Islamic countries, but in a Western, Christian nation like Britain? The Adhan has been heard in British towns and cities such as London, Cardiff, Peterborough, Edinburgh, Blackburn and many more. The

Adhan has even been heard in many small regional towns, such as Chelmsford in Essex. Applications to blare out the Adhan are regularly submitted across the United Kingdom, in towns that are too numerous to list here. Any objections to this alien-sounding Islamic tradition are condemned as 'Islamophobia'. One can only imagine the terrible fate that would await any Christian who was bold enough to ring church bells in Saudi Arabia.

In recent decades in Britain, the phenomenon of 'No-Go Zones' has surfaced in the media at regular intervals. From my own experience, an Islamic 'No-Go Zone' does not mean that a white British citizen would come to harm by simply walking through these areas. It does mean, however, that these 'No-Go Zones' are extremely hazardous for certain types of politics and that these areas are host to sky-high levels of extremism. Try walking down Bury Park in Luton with an English flag and you will see what I mean. Areas such as Bury Park, or Sparkbrook in Birmingham ('the jihadi capital of Britain'), or Whitechapel in East London, are notorious for Islamist extremism. Recently, a former Met Police detective, Peter Bleksley, took part in TV interviews and said, 'Let's tell the truth that many senior police officers and senior politicians won't. There are no-go areas in this country. They will all deny it. Everybody in the establishment will say this is not the fact. There are many areas in this country where the police are simply afraid to do their job. It has been born out numerous times by all the exploitation scandals that we have had of children in Rochdale and Rotherham. There are places where the police are very much afraid to tread.'

Elsewhere, a Tory MP by the name of Paul Scully, was recently quoted as saying, 'The point I am trying to make is if you look at parts of Tower Hamlets, for example, there are no-go areas. Parts of Birmingham, Sparkhill, where there are no-go areas, mainly because of doctrine, mainly because of people using, abusing in many ways, their religion because it is not the doctrine of Islam, to espouse what some of these people are saying. That, I think, is the concern that needs to be addressed.' Like a typical cowardly Tory, Scully apologised for his remarks after coming under pressure from the pro-Islam establishment. 'No-Go Zones' are not, therefore, local areas with 'checkpoints' that prevent non-Muslims from entering, but local areas that are dominated demographically by Muslims and that feature large contingents of radical Islamists that make entering that area dangerous and undesirable. British citizens across the country who live within close proximity to certain Muslim-dominated areas can vouch for the veracity of these statements. The only thing standing in the way of their recognition as 'No-Go Zones' is the left-wing, woke ideology of the political and media establishment who have their heads in the sand on this issue.

One particular nasty feature of these 'No-Go Zones' is the occasion appearance of 'Sharia Patrols', such as those that plagued East London in recent years. I personally led dozens of English activists into the heart of Whitechapel to try and combat these Sharia Patrols. We even had several decommissioned British Army snatch Land Rovers to ferry our activists around in safety. The Sharia Patrols in the East End of London were led by extremist Abdul Mahid, who I personally chased down the Bayswater Road screaming 'Terrorist!' at. The Sharia Patrols harassed revellers who were drinking alcohol in public and screamed abuse at homosexuals. They also told women to cover up. To oppose these Sharia Patrols, we launched our own 'Christian Patrols', hoping to go head-to-head with the Islamists on the streets of the East End. Of course, our Christian Patrols were condemned as 'Islamophobic'.

In recent years, Britain has seen an epidemic of 'Honour Killings', whereby female Muslims are murdered for bringing disrespect on their families by adopting Western customs, dress or by having relationships with non-Muslim Westerners. The number of Honour Killings is increasing rapidly. There are estimated to be dozens of Honour Killings in the UK every year. For example, a Muslim woman called Banaz Mahmod was murdered by her father and uncle for leaving an abusive marriage and falling in love with another man. Another example would be Samia Shahid, from Bradford, Yorkshire, who was killed on a trip to Pakistan by her ex-husband and father. The aim of Honour Killings is to 'restore honour' to a family name after a female member brings shame on the family by engaging in 'sinful' activity. To us Westerners, it is yet another example of the way women are treated as second-class citizens in Islam. Honour Killings are a stain on the cultural life of modern Britain. This barbaric practice is common among the medieval societies of the Middle East. It is a badge of shame that Honour Killings are becoming more commonplace in the United Kingdom.

As the strength and power of Islam in Britain grows, so do the calls for restrictions on free speech so that criticism of Islam is effectively made a criminal offence. Just recently, the new Labour government announced the creation of a 'Council on Islamophobia' to draft proposed new laws that will curtail any criticism of the religion. Labour is pandering to their voter base and do not care if these proposals will destroy freedom of expression in the UK. Britain will shortly join the ranks of barbaric, backward nations such as Pakistan and Saudi Arabia in outlawing criticism of Islam. These 'blasphemy laws' will soon become a reality of life in Britain if Labour has their way. It is a well-known feature of Islam that you cannot criticise the religion or the prophet Mohammed. The religious punishment for blasphemy is death. As Islam proliferates in Britain, so will draconian restrictions on free speech so that UK law falls in line with Sharia Law.

Another horrid aspect of Islam is the widespread practice of 'cousin marriage' within the UK. The problem is now so bad that it is receiving widespread media attention, even being debated in

Parliament. According to official statistics, up to 50% of all Islamic births in the UK are the result of cousin marriages. Inbreeding within the Islamic community is at debilitating levels. The children born from such unions are reaping the consequences of this practice of inbreeding, as you can imagine. Just recently, a Tory MP called Richard Holden introduced a proposal in Parliament to ban cousin marriages to reduce the level of Muslim inbreeding. He was fiercely opposed by Islamists and their supporters. One of those who spoke out against the proposal was Iqbal Mohamed, a Muslim member of Parliament who said that any such ban would be ineffective and that it ran contrary to Islamic culture. It seems, for the time being, that Muslims will continue to engage in catastrophic levels of inbreeding, leading to health complications and birth defects among their newborns.

As the number of Muslims increases across the land, so does the boisterousness of Muslim politics. I have always said that, with current population trends, Islam will become a major political force and will agitate and advocate in its own interests. I foresee a scenario in the future where Muslims make up a huge segment of our Parliament and will legislate in the interests of their own religion. This nightmare has started to unfold in recent years. Encouraged and facilitated by their allies on the far-left, pro-Palestine election candidates have emerged. In the general election of 2024, five of these openly Islamic candidates were elected to Parliament. Along with communist traitors such as Jeremy Corbyn, they have now formed a 'block' within Parliament to fight for the interests not of Britain or the British people, but for Islam and Palestine and the wider 'Ummah'. I envisage this block within Parliament to grow into a significant and powerful force, capable of passing laws exclusively for Islam. The success of Muslim politics has also been replicated at local council level, with dozens of Islamist candidates being elected to office around the country. In early 2025, known

Birmingham extremists Akhmed Yakoob and Shakeel Afsar announced a coalition of Islamic local election candidates called the 'Independent Candidate Alliance'. It must be remembered that the persons organising this new venture are not just 'independent candidates', they are overtly Islamic election candidates.

In response to the growing chorus among Muslims living in the UK that they turn to their own co-religionists in politics, the Labour party has embraced greater levels of appeasement and treachery. Firstly, Labour did an about-turn on the Israel-Hamas war, calling for a 'ceasefire' that would leave Hamas intact and able to commit further atrocities. Then Labour announced a crackdown on speech that Muslims do not like, leading to their 'Council on Islamophobia'. Labour is fast becoming the official and unabashed political representative of radical Islam in Britain.

Of course, the most appalling hallmark of Islam in Britain is regular and devastating terror attacks. Britain was regularly bombed by the IRA for decades, but this subsided long ago. Islamic terrorism has become so bad in Britain that when an attack occurs the authorities do their utmost to sweep it under the carpet, distort the narrative and hide the true motive of the attackers. The most obvious recent example is Southport, where the public was deliberately misled that the attacker was a quiet, Welsh Christian choir boy, when in fact, he was a sadistic, racist, murderous Islamist in possession of an Al Qaeda training manual. It will be too onerous to list in this chapter all the Islamic terror attacks that have plagued Britain since the early 2000s. Again, an examination of Islamic terrorism in Britain would require a book of its own. Significant and well-known Islamic attacks on Britain, carried out in the name of Allah, include the 7/7 suicide bombings in London, the Glasgow Airport attack, the slaughter of fusilier Lee Rigby in Woolwich, the Manchester Arena nail-bomb attack, the Westminster Bridge attack, the London Bridge and Borough Market attacks, the Parsons Green bombing, the Reading Park stabbings, the murder of David Amess MP and, of course, the Southport attack.

The number of foiled terror plots vastly outnumbers those that were realised. We are actually very fortunate to have such professional and efficient anti-terrorism police in the UK. I have personally been targeted by Islamic terrorists. A Muslim couple from Birmingham, Ummar Mirza and Madihah Taheer, who both supported ISIS, practiced chopping my head off on a gym dummy before being intercepted by anti-terror police. Had they carried out their dastardly plan, I would have been beheaded, ISIS style. Thankfully, they were neutralised before they could act. Quite unbelievably, Madihah Taheer (the female), has recently been released from prison, despite being found guilty of terrorism and conspiracy to commit attempted murder. She served around ten years in total. In 2020, the British security service 'MI5' confirmed that some 40,000 known wannabe-jihadists are on a 'terror watchlist'. They also confirmed that, due to a lack of resources, it is impossible to carry out surveillance on them. This is why so many terrorists who launch attacks are already 'known to the authorities'. The security services treat Islamists with kid gloves, deploying a softly-softly approach due to fear of being called 'racist' and being accused of 'targeting minorities'. As with so much in 'woke' modern Britain, political correctness trumps the safety and security of the public every time.

The political Left view Muslims as just another religious minority in need of protection and compassion. With this mindset, they gloss over or ignore all the hideous problems that Islam leaves in its wake. They hide the grooming gang scandals, they make excuses for Sharia Courts, they act as 'spin doctors' and apologists when terror attacks happen, they pander to extremists when they make demands, they install Muslims as candidates to utilise the 'Muslim block vote' (as they did in London with Sadiq Khan), and they label any opposition to Islamic extremism as 'Islamophobic'. Not many

Muslims in Britain would survive the 'Cricket Test' of being asked who they would support, England or Pakistan, when they watch a match between the two countries. Most Muslims would support Pakistan, not England, even though England is their new adoptive home. This applies even to those who were born in England. Many Muslims in Britain insist on celebrating Pakistan's 'Independence Day', and some Labour-run councils pander to this foreign nonsense by raising the flag of Pakistan on council offices in towns such as Rochdale. You will not catch many Muslims celebrating St George's Day or any native British traditions.

Far from being a 'minority community' comprised of fluffy bunnies and cute little kittens, Muslims in Britain harbour a range of extremist views that should cause extreme worry and consternation. A few examples will suffice. In 2006, a poll undertaken by NOP Research found that 45% of Muslims in the UK say that 9/11 was a conspiracy by the American and Israeli governments. The same poll found that 25% of Muslims believe that the 7/7 bombings were justified because the UK's support for American foreign policy. 75% of those Muslims who were questioned confirmed that Britain was 'not their country'. 30% of these Muslims confirmed they would prefer to live under Sharia Law and not British law. 28% of those surveyed expressed their desire for the UK to one day become a full Sharia compliant Islamic caliphate. 78% support punishments for anyone that publishes cartoons of the prophet Mohammed. 68% support criminal prosecutions of anyone who 'insults Islam'. All of these results are the product of a single survey carried out back in 2006.

According to a poll conducted in the wake of the 7th October 2023 attack in Israel, around 46% of those questioned supported Hamas, a proscribed terror group here in the UK. According to the same survey, only 25% agreed that Hamas committed murder and rape during the 7th October attack. Meanwhile, according to a poll conducted by JL Partners in 2024 found that one-third of Muslims in the UK said it was 'desirable' to implement 'Sharia Law' within the next two decades. I could continue to list opinion polls that back up my contention that Muslims in Britain harbour extremist views, but I feel that the examples above do the job and no further explanation is needed.

It must also be pointed out that all the negative issues outlined in this chapter, while focussed on Britain itself, could be transferred to any Western nation. We are all in the same boat facing the same problems. All Western nations have been subjected to endless waves of Islamic immigration, leading to terrorism, extremism, grooming gangs, no go zones, honour killings, political appeasement, the suppression of native criticism and opposition, and much more. Only the white European nations of Eastern Europe have managed to keep a lid on the problems associated with Islam. Russia, for example, has over twenty million Muslims, but does not tolerate extremism or petulant demands.

A detailed and forensic examination of Islam and its impact on Western nations in the modern era could easily be the subject of a huge and voluminous book of its own. I have tried my best to condense it into the length of a standard chapter, but it has not been easy. So much information has been left out while trying to compress it all into a single chapter, information that is critical to understanding Islam and its growth in the West. It is no surprise to me that this chapter is the longest, by far, of the whole book. But it was necessary, as I am sure you will appreciate.

In the final chapter of this book, I will examine what the future will look like if present trends continue. I will outline my personal beliefs of where our current 'multicultural experiment' will lead us if unchecked by a patriotic political revolution. I will forewarn you now, it will not a be an optimistic or uplifting look at a future that will be strewn with conflict and bloodshed. Nevertheless, we have to shake off any left-wing propagandistic sugar-coating and embrace a true awareness of just how terrible and barbarous that future will be. We cannot hide from it, as it awaits us over the horizon. A sober reflection of where we are heading is crucial if we are to mount a political fightback to reverse the situation.

11. Al-Malhama Al-Kubra

The conclusion of this book is simple, but stark. Unless the Christian West halts and reverses the tidal wave of Islamic mass immigration into our homelands, we will face the inevitable and certain prospect of a brutal civil war. The alternative is, as Colonel Gaddafi, said, that 'Allah will grant Islam victory in Europe—without swords, without guns, without conquest'. If you have read the entirety of this book and still think that Islam can peacefully co-exist with Western civilisation, then you need to go and re-read it from the beginning as you obviously haven't been paying attention.

Despite insistence to the contrary, there are only two states in Islam for humans, Muslim and non-Muslim. There is no neutral ground or grey area. You are either part of one, or part of the other. Islam even has special names for these two opposing camps. Muslims are believers, and constitute the 'Dar al-Islam', translated as the 'House of Islam'. All non-Muslims are part of the 'Dar al-Harb', which means the 'House of War'. It is pretty obvious why it is called the 'House of War', as it is the duty of all Muslims to wage war against the 'Dar al-Harb' until it is defeated. All non-Muslims the world over, all 7 billion of us, are part of the 'Dar al-Harb'. It is astonishing that a religion with billions of followers can be so brazen as to lump all non-believers into a camp called the House of War. It is even more astonishing that Western leaders thought it was a brilliant idea to import millions of people into our countries who follow such a religion.

There are at least 109 verses in the Quran that urge Muslims to make war against non-believers, many containing graphic details such as the chopping off of heads and fingers. Non-Muslims are a lesser people, according to the Quran. The Western world is learning the bitter truth that Islam cannot, and does not wish to, 'integrate' in any way. Be it bombings and acts of terror, attempts to create Sharia zones, blatant flouting of the law, or existing entirely within closed and insular communities, Islam remains hostile to our democratic, Western culture. In places where Islam rules, human rights, particularly for women, are all but non-existent. Wherever it goes, Islam strives to dominate. Islam does not become a part of a society but works to take over and become the whole of society. Those who are not Muslim are 'Khufar', non-believers, infidels, and heretics.

Women are afforded inferior status in Islamic society and their beating is authorised by the Quran. This point is regularly refuted by Muslims, but it is in the Quran in black and white and cannot be denied. Check out verse 4:34, 'Men are in charge of women by [right of] what Allah has given one over the other and what they spend [for maintenance] from their wealth. So righteous women are devoutly obedient, guarding in [the husband's] absence what Allah would have them guard. But those [wives] from whom you fear arrogance – [first] advise them; [then if they persist], forsake them in bed; and [finally], strike them. But if they obey you [once more], seek no means against them. Indeed, Allah is ever Exalted and Grand.' In other words, if your wife disobeys you, first refuse to have sex with them, and secondly, if they persist, 'strike' them. There is no other way to 'interpret' the word 'strike' that gives this verse another meaning. Islam is no friend to women.

Sir Winston Churchill himself had a word or two to say about the status of women in Islam. He wrote in his masterpiece, 'The River War' - after experiencing the full force of Islamic jihad in the Sudan - the following: 'The fact that in Mohammedan law every woman must belong to some man as his absolute property – either as a child, a wife, or a concubine – must delay the final extinction of slavery until the faith of Islam has ceased to be a great power among men.' Churchill was certainly not the last great stateman to comment on the inferior status of women in Islam.

It is worth examining what else Churchill had to say about the religion of Islam. Churchill was a prolific writer and authored dozens of books. He was also the great war leader that led the British Empire through its Darkest Hour in the Second World War. Churchill was a fierce opponent of what he called 'Mohammedanism'. This is the full quote from his book 'The River War', 'How dreadful are the curses which Mohammedanism lays on its votaries! Besides the fanatical frenzy, which is as dangerous in a man as hydrophobia in a dog, there is this fearful fatalistic apathy. The effects are apparent in many countries. Improvident habits, slovenly systems of agriculture, sluggish methods of commerce, and insecurity of property exist wherever the followers of the Prophet rule or live. A degraded sensualism deprives this life of its grace and refinement; the next of its dignity and sanctity.....Thousands become the brave and loyal soldiers of the faith: all know how to die but the influence of the religion paralyses the social development of those who follow it. No stronger retrograde force exists in the world. Far from being moribund, Mohammedanism is a militant and proselytising faith. It has already spread throughout Central Africa, raising fearless warriors at every step; and were it not that Christianity is sheltered in the strong arms of science, the science against which it had vainly struggled, the civilisation of modern Europe might fall, as fell the civilisation of ancient Rome.'

As can be seen here, Churchill plainly wrote that Islam is as dangerous in a human as rabies is in a dog. He goes on to describe how Islam 'paralyses' the social development of any society, something we see in abundance all across the world in the modern era. Churchill describes Islam as a 'retrograde force'. Churchill deduces that if Western civilisation was not scientifically more advanced than Islam, then 'the civilisation of modern Europe might fall'. I doubt very much that Churchill would ever believe that one day long after his death his beloved England would be in danger of becoming an Islamic nation thanks to the treachery of generations of self-serving career politicians. Churchill was no doubt influenced at a young age of the legendary leader of the British Liberal Party, Sir William Gladstone. During the late Victorian era, Gladstone held the Quran above his head in Parliament and said, 'So long as there is this book, there will be no peace in the world.' Islam has also been the favourite of tyrants and dictators, due to its aggressive and warlike nature. Adolf Hitler said the following of Islam, 'You see, it's been our misfortune to have the wrong religion. Why didn't we have the religion of the Japanese, who regard sacrifice for the Fatherland as the highest good? The Mohammedan religion [Islam] too would have been more compatible to us than Christianity. Why did it have to be Christianity with its meekness and flabbiness?'

Faced with the complete failure of Islam to advance human civilisation over a period of 1,400 years, Muslim apologists will always make tenuous references to the 'Islamic Golden Age' that came in the wake of their conquests of the Middle East. However, the term 'Islamic Golden Age' is fraudulent and misleading. Wikipedia describes it like this: 'The Islamic Golden Age was a period of scientific, economic, and cultural flourishing in the history of Islam, traditionally dated from the 8th century to the 13th century.' The so-called Islamic Golden Age was not a flowering of Islamic science and progress - what in fact occurred was the opposite. Islamic armies invaded and conquered advanced regions such as ancient Babylonian, Syria and Persia and found great scientific and technological literature within these lands which they then adopted as their own. It is no coincidence that the period 'the 8th century to the 13th century' is one of relentless Islamic conquest.

The true source of all of the scientific advances made during the so-called 'Islamic Golden Age' were not Islamic, but the product of prior ancient civilisations. Islam simply claimed the achievements of other societies and made them their own. In other words, they regurgitated the science and accomplishments of others. Even the styles of art and decorations on Islamic buildings were originally not Islamic. Islamic 'art' on famous buildings, such as the Dome of the Rock in Jerusalem, is a mixture of Greek, Roman, early Christian, Byzantine, Central Asian, Chinese and the Sassanian art of pre-Islamic Persia. If you remove the 'Islamic Golden Age' from the historical timeline, then Islam has failed to progress at all. It is ideologically stuck in the 7th Century world and value system in which it began. This is why true Islamic societies, such as the recent ISIS caliphate in Syria and Iraq, and Afghanistan under the Taliban, for example, are so backward.

With all of the above in mind, we can confidently say that Islam has never managed to advance or progress humanity – instead, it has degraded the regions in which it holds sway. As Churchill said, it is a true 'retrograde force'. If current demographic trends across the West continue and are not reversed, then Europe will become fully Islamic at some point. High Islamic birthrates, coupled with mass immigration, will easily outdo the disastrously low birthrates of modern Europeans. You cannot overcome mathematics. Colonel

Gaddafi will undoubtedly be proven correct within our lifetimes unless things change radically across the Western world.

Which brings us to an important question. Why did I choose as the title of this book, 'The Final Battle'. As I have already explained, Islam and the West have been at war, on and off, since the 7th Century. But now, faced with an immense immigration invasion and demographic disaster, we are fast approaching 'The Final Battle'. The Bible describes the final battle at the end of the world as 'Armageddon'. In Christian belief, Armageddon will be the last battle between good and evil before the Day of Judgement. Muslims have a similar belief and theology. The Islamic term for the final battle is 'Al-Malhama Al-Kubra', which translates as 'The Greatest Battle'. Al-Malhama Al-Kubra' will be an apocalyptic war that is prophesied to take place at the end of the world.

Whether you subscribe to 'Armageddon' or 'Al-Malhama Al-Kubra', only a fool would deny that the West and Islam are heading towards a titanic clash that will decide the fate of the world. There can only be two outcomes. Either Christianity will fight back, survive and turn the tide, or Islam will finally crush the 'Dar al-Harb' and the West will fall. The fate of the Western world hangs by a thread. This book is my humble attempt to bring this 1,400-year interminable conflict to the attention of modern readers. We must prepare ourselves for the coming 'Al-Malhama Al-Kubra' and arm ourselves with a deep knowledge of our civilisational enemy. Either the West makes a stand, or Islam will be our future. It is up to each of us to decide whether we fight back politically or capitulate.

Make your decision....

Printed in Great Britain
by Amazon

60824399R00070